The Orange Way

A Long Distance Walk following the
march of Prince William of Orange
from Brixham to London
in 1688

Route described in both directions

With historical commentary

by Leslie Ham

Meridian Books

Published 2003 by Meridian Books

© Leslie Ham 2003

ISBN 1-869922-47-6

Meridian Books
40 Hadzor Road, Oldbury, West Midlands B68 9LA

Printed in Great Britain by Franklin Publicity, Macclesfield

Contents

Preface

by Ann Holt

Walking has its own history. Its historians try to answer such questions as why and how walking became a recreation in its own right when it is, at its most simple level, just a means of getting from one place to another. They look at the consequences of walking having become a recreation, the struggles over footpaths and rights of access, the court cases, the campaigns for new legislation, the formation of distinctive organisations for and representing walkers. They also try to discern what sort of people walkers were, what their attitudes were, what it was about their ideas and interests which made walking so important to them.

One of the answers to the last question is that many walkers have been particularly interested in the experience of exploring history on foot. Walking lends itself to being combined with other interests, that is part of its charm. Plants, birds, geology, archaeology, landscape, writing, painting and drawing, as well as history and no doubt many other subjects have all, over the years, been grist to the walker's mill. The romantic movement in thought and art which changed the way people looked at the countryside encouraged, though it did not invent, an interest in the traces of former times and walking has often been the best, and sometimes the only, way of exploring these traces. Such explorations often required a good deal of hardihood on the part of the walker. William Hutton, a Birmingham businessman, amateur historian and walker, once commented 'an antiquary does not deserve the name who cannot fast half a day, and live hard the other half ... I trust for drink till I meet with a spring or an alehouse'. But Hutton was one of those epic walkers who were such a feature of the eighteenth and nineteenth centuries. Among other exploits he boasted of having climbed Snowdon, in 1799, at the age of seventy-six. Those following Leslie Ham's route can be assured of a much easier time.

For many walkers the attraction of the past has been what could be seen, of being amongst the ruined castles and standing stones, which evoke the mystery of the passage of time. But visible signs of the past have never been essential for anyone with imagination. In youth Walter Scott used to make excursions with a group of friends from his home in Edinburgh. The friends were mainly interested in romantic, mountainous scenery, preferably enhanced by a castle, but Scott had equal pleasure in places where remarkable historical events had happened. His companions were not particularly sympathetic towards his preference for wandering the site of the battle of Bannockburn over viewing the landscape from the battlements of Stirling Castle. But later on his ability to commune with the past was to open its romance to generations of readers. As history became part of the stock in trade of guidebook writers and tourists, so it did that of walkers and writers of walking guides.

There is yet another dimension to the walker's relationship with history. The fact that public rights of way are customary rights, which until relatively recently had to be proved to be public by attempting to show that they had been used as such from 'a time beyond which the memory of man goeth not' has tended to draw the attention of walkers to the ancient lineage of the ways they use. Age and traditional usage was what made a route open to all as of right. It is not surprising that the two earliest-known footpath protection societies, founded in 1824 and 1826, included the phrase 'ancient footpaths' in their titles.

This sense of the way itself having a history has encouraged many to see themselves as only part of a great procession of walkers and other travellers, using ancient routes for a vast variety of errands. The road built by Rome's legions may have become a simple footpath from nowhere in particular to nowhere in particular, but the habit of using it established and maintained the right to use it as its character and purpose changed. Hilaire Belloc mused over this continuity of use when writing about the Pilgrims' Way from Winchester to Canterbury, a medieval Christian pilgrimage route grafted seamlessly onto a road already old, with some of its pre-Christian significance lingering on in the folk memory. His imaginary pilgrim is advised to pass a sacred well and climb an isolated hill from which spirits were banished by the faith, and where martyrs died, and to take care not to neglect the stone, 'whose virtue saved our fathers in the great battle'.

William of Orange's advance to London may not have the same mystical qualities, but he and his men certainly used the roads, paths and tracks familiar to generations before them, including other armies, politicians and people driven by the desire for a better, according to their lights, society. The revolution of 1688 seems very foreign to us now, its anti-Catholic rhetoric jarring against modern attempts to treat the beliefs of others with the respect we would wish for our own. But it was a different world, marked by the upheavals of the Reformation and the Civil War. England's power-holders were turning decisively from one interpretation of the Christian faith to another, from one set of political alliances to another and, eventually, towards a more democratic view of the role of the individual in society. As you follow Leslie Ham's route you will cross and re-cross the footprints of history. As Edward Thomas once wrote, 'tread softly because your way is over men's dreams'.

Ann Holt is a freelance researcher who is particularly interested in the history of walking as a recreation. She has contributed articles to several journals, including *The Rambler* and *The Rights of Way Review*, and compiled a number of historical reports for The Ramblers' Association. She is currently writing a book on the history of walking.

Introduction

The concept

This guidebook is intended for those walkers who not only enjoy walking for walking's sake but would also wish to have their pleasure enhanced by the knowledge that they are walking a route of English history. My objective was to create a long distance path across the southern counties of England encompassing a route that would allow us to walk in the footsteps history. This ideal led me to research the route of the March of Prince William of Orange and his army from Brixham to London in 1688. Here is a route that encompasses a reminder of England's heritage, which together with its long distance route would satisfy both objectives. The heady days of the Glorious Revolution and to follow its route across the English countryside from the shores of Devon to the great city of London is to live its history. Most National Trails or long distance paths are often across hills, ridges, woods or broad tracts of land as to be far from accommodation and transport. My route by comparison crosses many rivers, great plains, over hills, and through town and village but is never far from an overnight hostelry, railway station or bus routes and does not require awkward positioning walks to join or exit the route. It has contained within each section, the unfolding story of the Glorious Revolution, highlighting the relevant events, which took place on or near the route.

The style

Although the route is over 560kms (350 miles) long each way, I have divided it into fifteen sections, and sub-sections within it of easy length to accommodate various types of walker, and allowing for the varying methods of joining and leaving the route. For those who wish just to walk short distances can do so and still gain the pleasure of walking in history. It is possible to join or leave the walk at intermediate points within a section. I have shown a table of cumulative distances to give the walker an easy method of calculating distances and times to and from places within or across sections. Those who wish to cover greater distances can readily combine sections. For those who wish to complete a continuous walk of the whole route will find that it lends itself admirably for that achievement.

In this third millennium and age of the Internet and mobile telephone I have geared the information contained in this book to take account of the increasing number of people who would wish to interrogate the Net for any information they need to know regarding accommodation, or transportation timetables. To facilitate a more useful system I have included information, where more detailed information can be obtained, rather than to clog up the book with too much little used knowledge. Hence the Tourist Information Centres I have listed, will, I hope, be of more use than lists of recommended B & B's. More walkers today carry mobile telephones with them and to satisfy those who wish to organize as they go I have included the essential telephone numbers to assist them. The section information, I hope, gives helpful information to assist with planning your walk. A few words of explanation regarding their definitions:

Route	means the full extent of this section of the route.
Map	gives the recommended walking maps that cover this section of the route, although some sections could be completed without maps, e.g. following a canal or river for the whole section.
Start	gives the exact starting point of this section of the route.
Finish	gives the exact finishing point of this section of the route.
Distance	gives the distance from start to finish of this section.
Time	means an average walking time for this section excluding stops, in decimal hours.
Transport:	gives the points at which it is possible to use public transport.
Place of historical interest:	means a place nearby, which has some connection with Prince William or his army.
Special notes	means there is something particular that you should take into consideration.
The history	means the events that took place on or near the route in that section.
Eastbound	means the basic route direction of the walk from west to east (Brixham to London).
Westbound	means the basic route direction of the walk from east to west (London to Brixham).

Where I have referred to navigational information within a section this has been initially established 'in the field'. The distances have sometimes been measured by pedometer, grid references have been established with a GPS system and bearings have been established by compass. All these details have been additionally map checked separately to eliminate errors.

Distances are recorded to give a good idea of where to look out for the next navigational point and are not intended to be accurate to the last metre, but nevertheless great care has been taken to establish them accurately. Primarily these distances have been established in metric, as there is not a major problem treating metres and yards as roughly the same up to 1km. Distances over 1km have been additionally converted to imperial and rounded to the nearest quarter mile for those who prefer old money.

The hand-drawn sketch maps are noted in the text at the point in which the route description can first be identified on the appropriate map. This convention has been applied to both directions of the route description.

I have chosen to divide the route into sections of unequal length merely to facilitate a more suitable start and finish point for transport and accommodation purposes although it is possible to obtain transport at points mentioned in between. It was never the intention that walkers should necessarily walk a full section on one day if it were outside their capabilities, or indeed, a weather window or a shorter winter's day.

The history

As with most Revolutions bloodless or not, there are invariably many underlying causes, both major and minor. The causation events, in time add up to an intoleration of a situation and a desire for change. In the long term progressive changes might pacify but a short-term response usually means revolution.

The events that led up to Prince William's army landing on the shores of the West Country were, in the main, matters of religion, and particularly Roman Catholic encroachment into the higher echelons of public life in England. During James II's brief reign from 1685 to 1688, himself a Catholic, had insisted upon placing Catholics into prominent positions of authority, civil and military, much against the will of the populace and at variance with Protestants and the Anglican Church of England. In parts of the army many Protestant officers and soldiers were dismissed, drafts of Catholic soldiers were sent to England from Ireland.

When the drift from Protestantism to Catholicism, together with James' arbitrary measures became intolerable, his subjects turned to Protestant Prince William of Orange to save their rights and liberties. Prince William, who had earlier married Mary, herself a Protestant and the daughter of James II, accepted the call sent him and with his army and a 'Protestant wind' landed at Torbay on the 5th November 1688. He came ashore at Brixham from the ship 'Brill' carried aloft by a local fisherman Peter Varwell to proclaim 'the liberties of England and the Protestant religion I will maintain'. Prince William had come ashore with approximately 15,500 soldiers and up to 4000 horses. The Rev Gilbert Burnet Bishop of Salisbury is more precise and claims the figure to be 14,352. So began the Bloodless or Glorious Revolution, at times not quite bloodless, ending some 44 days later on the 18th December, in London, King James II having fled, and William riding from Windsor to lodge at St James's Palace by that same evening. King James having been forced to take early retirement faired better than his father Charles I, who had been forced to take severance in its most severe form.

The route

This long distance path inasmuch as is possible or feasible, follows the route taken by Prince William of Orange and his army from Brixham to London in 1688. The March passed through towns and villages across the southern counties of England. The army marched in three divisions, each division being a day or so behind the other. Prince William usually moved with his guard amidst the second division but on occasions diverted to make personal visits to the local supportive aristocracy along the way.

The three armies moved on a wide front along a main route, camping in the surrounding villages and on occasions covering a 30/50-kilometre (20/30 miles) area in circumference. Studying various writings both contemporary and more recent publications, it is possible to establish most of the places that Prince William or his army visited on their route to London, some writings are more detailed than others are.

It is not feasible or desirable to visit every place that William or his army passed through, as with the route from Exeter to Honiton. William's likely route would today pass by Exeter airport with few public footpaths. Alternative possible and more interesting routes have been taken directly from Topsham where William's heavy ordnance came ashore.

Similarly between Windsor and Syon House, Brentford I have chosen to take a route using the Grand Union Canal rather than try to seek a route past the now industrial complexes surrounding London Airport. Bearing this in mind I have stayed generally with the main route of the army or followed Prince William himself in some instances, particularly to Abingdon. Passing through modern developments road walking has, where possible, been kept to a minimum. In some areas particularly in parts of the West Country, lane walking is unavoidable, but not unpleasant. This always has to be balanced with the knowledge of knowing that one is walking in the footsteps of Prince William of Orange and the Glorious Revolution.

The route can be walked at any colour of the year – snowdrops – daffodils – roses – autumn leaves.

Enjoy the walk.

Some basic information

Maps and navigational equipment

Please do carry the appropriate map and a compass, a GPS might be useful. Within each section of the walk I have indicated which OS maps it would be best to use. The hand drawn sketch maps have been placed closest to the appropriate text and mainly in the Eastbound sections.

Clothing and equipment

The Orange Way path can be walked at any time of the year – the author walked in spring, summer, autumn and winter. It has to be said that to walk in the winter especially in the West Country needs the best weather protection clothing. In some cases the wearing of waterproof 'green wellies' in poor weather would be a distinct advantage on some sections (see below).

Accommodation

I have listed telephone numbers of the Tourist Information Centres to assist walkers with finding accommodation rather than clogging up the book with lists recommended of B&B's.

Transport

The telephone numbers of rail and bus companies along or near the route are listed. In the event of you wishing to use a transport service noted as infrequent, please check the timings with the relevant bus company before setting out as some villages are only served by shopping or school buses to the nearest town. There are plenty of car parks and locations for cars at various places along the route but be careful when hoping to leave a car parked on a narrow country lane, as tractors frequently need to pass by.

Refreshments

There are many pubs, cafes or restaurants along the route for full meals or snacks and rather than list them I have chosen to do the opposite and make special note if a particular section has a scarcity where it is advisable to carry ones own supplies. There are plenty of 'Kiddleywinks' in the West Country. I have assumed that walkers would always carry water and emergency food supplies in any event.

Footpaths

Footpaths across farmland and fields have been described as per the relevant OS map or on the ground waymarks. At crop times some of these footpaths maybe obscured by crops, or in other places maybe you will find an additional electric fences placed across a field path to contain livestock. Although most farmers indicate an alternative route around the field, occasionally some do not. In places where it is not possible to follow the line of the path please detour round the problem as best as is possible. Fortunately these problems are quite rare. You may feel like mentioning the worst cases of unnecessary obstruction to the local County Council Rights of Way office to ease the problem for future walkers. Addresses and contact telephone numbers are listed in this book. Indeed most Councils have websites where you can email your observations. Having said this I have found farmers to be most helpful to walkers, their local knowledge is invaluable. Do not be afraid to knock on farmhouse doors and ask for guidance, you may even get tea and sympathy.

Safety

Please be aware that sometimes this route will cross over busy main roads, use country lanes or follow the course of rivers and streams. Take care when crossing roads and walk along country lanes in a manner where drivers in both directions can see you best. On occasions the route crosses military areas, please keep to the designated footpaths and read the posted warning notices regarding any objects found on the ground.

Sections

Section 1 Brixham to Newton Abbot

Section 2 Newton Abbot to Exeter

Section 3 Exeter to Honiton

Section 4 Honiton to Beaminster

Section 5 Beaminster to Sherborne

Section 6 Sherborne to Wincanton

Section 7 Wincanton to Hindon

Section 8 Hindon to Salisbury

Section 9 Salisbury to Burbage

Section 10 Burbage to Newbury

Section 11 Newbury to Abingdon

Section 12 Abingdon to Reading

Section 13 Reading to Windsor

Section 14 Windsor to Brentford

Section 15 Brentford to St James's Palace

Route Calculator

	Distances		Times	Cumulative		
	Kms	Miles	Hours	Kms	Miles	Hours
Section 1						
Brixham Harbour to Higher Yalberton	11.0	7.0	3.0	11.0	7.0	3.0
Higher Yalberton to Berry Pomeroy	5.6	3.5	1.5	16.6	10.5	4.5
Berry Pomeroy to Ipplepen	9.0	5.5	3.0	25.6	16.0	7.5
Ipplepen to Abbotskerwell	4.0	2.5	1.0	29.6	18.5	8.5
Abbotskerwell to Newton Abbot	4.0	2.5	1.25	33.6	21.0	9.75
Section 2						
Newton Abbot to Chudleigh	12.5	7.75	3.0	46.1	28.75	12.75
Chudleigh to Shillingford St George	10.5	6.5	2.5	56.6	35.25	15.25
Shillingford St George to Exminster	5.5	3.5	1.5	62.1	38.75	16.75
Exminster to Exeter	9.5	6.0	2.5	71.6	44.75	19.25
Section 3						
Exeter to Topsham	8.0	5.0	2.0	79.6	49.75	21.25
Topsham to Woodbury	7.1	4.5	1.75	86.7	54.25	23.0
Woodbury to Harpford Bridge	11.5	7.25	3.25	98.2	61.5	26.25
Harpford Bridge to Ottery St Mary	6.5	4.0	1.75	104.7	65.5	28.0
Ottery St Mary to Honiton	12.2	7.5	3.0	116.9	73.0	31.0
Section 4						
Honiton to Axminster	17.0	10.5	5.0	133.9	83.5	36.0
Axminster to Hawkchurch	6.3	4.0	2.0	140.2	87.5	38.0
Hawkchurch to Sadborow Pound	5.5	3.5	1.5	145.7	91.0	39.5
Sadborow Pound to Pilsdon Pen	6.2	4.0	2.0	151.9	95.0	41.5
Pilsdon Pen to Beaminster	9.5	6.0	2.5	161.4	101.0	44.0
Section 5						
Beaminster to Mosterton	6.0	3.75	1.5	167.4	104.75	45.5
Mosterton to Crewkerne	5.5	3.5	1.5	172.9	108.25	47.0
Crewkerne to Haselbury Plucknett	4.2	2.5	1.0	177.1	110.75	48.0
Haselbury Plucknett to East Coker	9.0	5.5	2.25	186.1	116.25	50.25
East Coker to Bradford Abbas	6.6	4.0	1.5	192.7	120.25	51.75
Bradford Abbas to Sherborne	6.0	3.75	1.5	198.7	124.0	53.25
Section 6						
Sherborne to Goathill	5.0	3.0	1.25	203.7	127.0	54.5
Goathill to Crendle Corner	2.1	1.25	0.5	205.8	128.25	55.0
Crendle Corner to Yenston	6.2	3.75	1.5	212.0	132.0	56.5
Yenston to Kington Magna	6.8	4.25	1.75	218.8	136.25	58.25
Kington Magna to Wincanton	10.0	6.25	2.5	228.8	142.5	60.75
Section 7						
Wincanton to Zeals	9.3	5.75	2.5	238.1	148.25	63.25
Zeals to Mere	4.1	2.5	1.0	242.2	150.75	64.25
Mere to Hindon	10.9	6.75	2.75	253.1	157.5	67.0
Section 8						
Hindon to Dinton	12.2	8.0	3.25	265.3	165.5	70.25
Dinton to Salisbury	17.5	10.75	4.5	282.8	176.25	74.75

	Distances		Times	Cumulative		
	Kms	Miles	Hours	Kms	Miles	Hours
Section 9						
Salisbury to Amesbury	16.3	10.0	4.0	299.6	186.5	78.75
Amesbury to Netheravon via Stonehenge	13.5	8.5	3.5	312.6	194.75	82.25
Netheravon to Everleigh	9.2	5.75	2.5	321.8	200.5	84.75
Everleigh to Collingbourne Kingston	5.6	3.5	1.5	327.4	204.0	86.25
Section 10						
Collingbourne Kingston to Burbage	7.0	4.25	1.75	334.4	208.25	88.0
Burbage to Savernake Forest	7.8	4.75	2.0	342.2	213.0	90.0
Savernake Forest to Ramsbury	9.5	6.0	2.5	351.7	219.0	92.5
Ramsbury to Hungerford	8.5	5.25	2.5	360.2	224.25	95.0
Hungerford to Newbury	14.0	8.75	3.5	374.2	233.0	98.5
Section 11						
Newbury to Chieveley	9.2	5.75	2.5	383.4	238.75	101.0
Chieveley to West Ilsley	10.0	6.25	2.5	393.4	245.0	103.5
West Ilsley to Steventon	11.5	7.25	3.0	404.9	252.25	106.5
Steventon to Abingdon	8.8	5.5	2.0	413.7	257.75	108.5
Section 12						
Abingdon to Day's Lock (Dorchester)	12.8	8.0	3.25	426.5	265.75	111.75
Day's Lock (Dorchester) to Wallingford	8.6	5.25	2.25	435.1	271.0	114.0
Wallingford to Goring .	10.8	6.75	2.75	445.9	277.75	116.75
Goring to Whitchurch	7.1	4.5	1.75	453.0	282.25	118.5
Whitchurch to Reading	10.6	6.5	2.75	463.6	288.75	121.25
Section 13						
Reading to Sonning	5.7	3.5	1.5	469.3	292.25	122.75
Sonning to Henley	10.0	6.25	2.5	479.3	298.5	125.25
Henley to Aston	5.1	3.25	1.25	484.4	301.75	126.5
Aston to Marlow	9.5	6.0	2.5	493.9	307.75	129.0
Marlow to Maidenhead	12.8	8.0	3.25	506.7	315.75	132.25
Maidenhead to Windsor	10.0	6.25	2.5	516.7	322.0	134.75
Section 14						
Windsor to West Drayton	14.0	8.75	3.5	530.7	330.75	138.25
West Drayton to Brentford	12.0	7.5	3.0	542.7	338.25	141.25
Section 15						
Brentford to Hammersmith	12.0	7.5	3.0	554.7	345.75	144.25
Hammersmith to St James's Palace	8.0	5.0	2.0	562.7	350.75	146.25

The above data can be used to establish the length of any intermediate walk together with its timings e.g. If you wanted to walk from Ipplepen to Exminster or vice versa, deduct the cumulative data at Ipplepen from the cumulative data at Exminster as follows:

	Kms	Miles	Hours
Cumulative data at Exminster (destination)	62.1	38.75	16.75
Cumulative data at Ipplepen (destination)	25.6	16.0	7.5
Distance/Hours from Ipplepen to Exminster	36.5	22.75	9.25

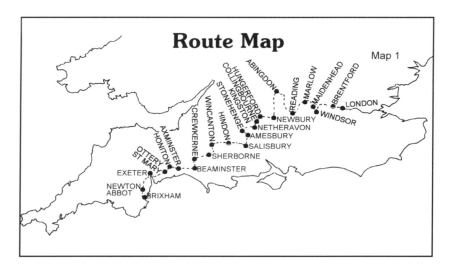

Acknowledgments

Berkshire County Council
Devon County Council
Dorset County Council
Oxfordshire County Council
Somerset County Council
Wiltshire County Council
Local history groups
Ramblers Association
National Picture Gallery
British Library
Public Record Office, Kew
Ann Holt, for the Preface

Nick Hance MBE, Public Relations Manager, UKAEA
Arthur Hart, for assistance with photography
Peter Groves – my publisher, for help and assistance through the publishing process
Route checkers: Arthur Amos; John Betteridge; Keith Brown; Derek & Joan Crosbee; Jim Fewkes; Paul James; Tim Lowe; Jean Mills; Derek Purcell; Elizabeth Stein; Ken Tatum, Tourist Information Centres

Publishers' Note

Every care has been taken in the preparation of this book. The walk has been independently checked and is believed to be correct at the time of publication. However, no guarantee can be given that it contains no errors or omissions and neither the author nor the publishers can accept any responsibility for loss, damage or inconvenience resulting from the use of this book.

Please remember that the countryside is continually changing: hedges and fences may be removed or re-sited; footbridges and river banks may suffer flood damage; footpaths may be re-routed or ploughed over and not reinstated (as the law requires); concessionary paths may be closed. If you do encounter any such problems please let the publishers know, and please report any obstructions to rights of way to the relevant local authority.

About the Author

A resident of Weybridge for over 30 years now, Leslie Ham was born in Burnley, Lancashire in 1938. He spent his formative years in Blackpool but has also lived in Kirkham, Hucknall, Nottingham, Derby, Blackburn and several locations in West London. From 1957 he spent two years doing his National Service in Aldershot, Cyprus and Jordan. In 1960 he joined BOAC, which later merged with BEA to become British Airways and spent a total of thirty-five interesting years at London Airport.

His interest in walking began in the 1960s in the North Downs, later completing many of the Long Distance footpaths in Southern England. These included the South Downs Way, North Downs Way, Thames Path, Ridgeway, Vanguard Way, Greensand Way, Thames Valley Heritage Walk, London Countryside Way and several canal-side routes. Abroad he has trekked on five Continents, including the Himalayas, New Zealand, China, South Africa, mainland France, Corsica, Patagonia, Peru and Bolivia. He has a desire to walk on the sixth Continent.

Photo: A Hart

In addition to walking his other main interests include travel, photography, history, genealogy, archeology, music, poetry, modern art, target shooting, computers and anything art deco.

Since he took early retirement in 1995 he has thoroughly enjoyed his freedom and concentrated on the above with difficulty. He decided to write a walking guidebook with a historical theme thereby combining two of his interests. He found the writing of *The Orange Way* a fascinating project and learned a great deal about many things, particularly the countryside and its problems.

Leslie is investigating a further project for another walking guidebook also with a historical theme.

Prince William's Personal History

William III of Orange Stuart King of England
Birth: 14 Nov 1650, The Hague, Netherlands
Mother: Mary Stuart, Princess Royal
Father: Prince William II of Orange
Marriage: 4 Nov 1677, St James's Palace, London – to Mary daughter of the Duke of York, later James II
Died: 8 Mar 1702, Kensington Palace, London
Buried: Westminster Abbey, London

William III

Artist unknown
© *National Portrait Gallery*

William of Orange, posthumous son of William II of Orange ruler of the United Netherlands, who by birth (being the grandson of Charles I) and marriage, with Mary, heiress presumptive of the English Crown daughter of James, Duke of York and by his position as Champion of Protestantism on the Continent, and as the great opponent of Louis XIV, was naturally interested in English affairs but finally came to loggerheads, James complaining that the disaffected fugitives from England were harboured in Holland, and that the Prince corrupted the English regiments in the Dutch service; while William accused the King of a design to pass over Mary in favour of Anne, (who it was reported, was ready, in that case to turn Papist).

William was of medium height, thin with ungainly limbs and stooping shoulders: forehead ample: nose high and aquiline: lips thin and close set: countenance pale and haggard, but lit up by keen eagle eyes, weak and delicate in frame and a martyr to chronic asthma; yet capable of enduring any amount of fatigue and privation, and extremely fond of athletic exercise, in which he greatly excelled. His family Nassau was unhealthy and suffered from fevers of a tubercular nature. William was always weak and had a constant consumptive cough. His face was sullen and bloodless and scored with deep lines, which were the product of fighting ceaseless pain. He could not handle a horse or sword until full grown. His success in life came from the care he took to eat simple, drink little and obtain plenty of sleep. Nonetheless he overcame all of

Descendants of James I

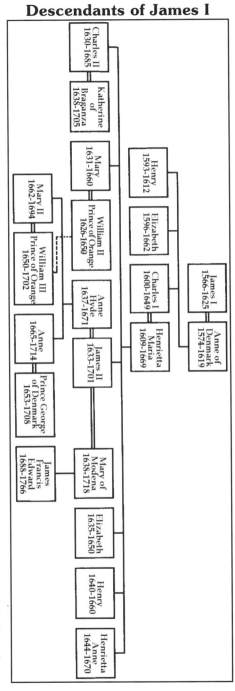

these physical setbacks to present a dashing and inspiring figure on horseback in the thick of the fight.

He had no taste for literature, art or science, his attainment consisting of those subjects (e.g. language and mathematics), that could be turned to account in war.

Genealogy of the Stuarts

James I   1603-1625
Charles I   1625-1649

Interregnum 1649-1660

Charles II   1660-1685
James II   1685-1688
William III   1689-1702
Anne   1702-1714

The Courageous Soldiers of the West

Now to maintain the Protestant cause,
All the whole West does loyally stand,
For our lives, religion and laws,
Roman shall never reign in this land.
Stout lads brisk and airy, for William and Mary,
They'll valiantly fight their rights to maintain.

Bridgewater boys I needs must commend,
Freely they to the wars did repair,
Parents and wife, nay, every friend,
They commended to heaven's great care;
Life and fortune freely venter,
Nothing alive true courage and stain.
Stout lads brisk and airy, for William and Mary,
They'll valiantly fight their rights to maintain.

As for the town brave Taunton-dean,
Their loyalty shall ne'er be forgot,
For our most gracious king and his queen,
They will engage with thundering shot.
Noble true souls came flocking amain.
Stout lads brisk and airy, for William and Mary,
They'll valiantly fight their rights to maintain.

Section 1
Brixham to Newton Abbot

Map: OS Outdoor Leisure 20, OS Explorer 110
Start: William of Orange statue Brixham Harbour
Finish: Railway Station Newton Abbot
Distance: 33.6kms (21.0 miles)
Time: 9.75 hrs
Transport: Railway: Churston, Newton Abbot
     Buses: Brixham, (Churston, Galmpton Infrequent), A385 at
Longcombe Cross, Ipplepen, Abbotskerwell (Infrequent), Newton Abbot
Place of historical interest: Brixham harbour and statue to Prince William,
Furzeham Common, Yalberton King William's Cottage, Longcombe Parliament,
Berry Pomeroy Castle, Commemorative stone St Leonard's Tower Newton
Abbot, Forde House Newton Abbot.

The History

On the 5ᵗʰ November 1688 Prince William came ashore at Brixham and is said to have spent his first night in the house of one Peter Varwell, a local fisherman who lived in Middle St, Brixham. His troops unloaded from over 400 ships of the Dutch fleet and stationed themselves on the high ground behind the town known as Furzeham Common where they spent a cold wet night being wary of an attack by James's forces, but they were mainly still in Salisbury at this time. The Prince's 4000 horses came ashore the following day.

The famous 'Protestant wind' which had blown them down the Channel had kept the English navy locked in the Thames Estuary and unable to counter Prince William's move. From the outset Prince William had some serious concerns, firstly, financial difficulties, secondly, organization of resistance to King James in an area under his control, thirdly, the prospect of actual combat with the loyal army, and fourthly, the transfer of authority from the lawful head of government to himself. The financial difficulties gave him an immediate problem of paying his own army and the purchase of food and fodder, which were partly solved when he reached Exeter where he took over the tax machinery. Actual combat with King James's army never materialized. Had James' army been

Statue of William, Brixham Harbour
Photo: A Hart

on hand in the Torbay area when Prince William landed, it would have been a relatively easy task to defeat his seasick army who were suffering badly from many days of being aboard their ships waiting for a favourable wind.

A commemorative statue of Prince William is erected by the harbour at Brixham. The inscription carved on its side reads as follows:

William
Prince of Orange
afterwards
William III
King of Great Britain & Ireland
landed near this spot
5th November 1688
and issued his famous declaration
'The Liberties of England
and
the Protestant religion
I will maintain'

Prince William had landed with 15,500 troops and 4000 horses, King James's standing army was about 35,000. The poor state of the roads in the West Country made transportation slow and difficult, and William's army had to rely on local packhorses and carts to transport their baggages along the narrow lanes. His armies advanced, some along the coast to Paignton and Newton Abbot, while others went by the hinterland by way of Churston, Yalberton, Longcombe, Berry Pomeroy, Ipplepen, Abbotskerwell and then to Newton Abbot.

At Yalberton there still stands a cottage known as King William's Cottage where the Prince rested and dined on his way to Longcombe. At Longcombe there is another cottage called 'Parliament', which stands as a reminder of the place of the first so called Parliament, held by William on English soil. Here he met Sir Edward Seymour of nearby Berry Pomeroy who earlier had been ousted from his position of Recorder of Totnes to make way for a Catholic by order of King James. Prince William's outriders were sent ahead to search for weapons in the houses of Catholics.

The Devonian weather was at its worst. The Reverend John Whittle, Chaplain to Prince William who travelled with the army records a night in the open thus:

'The Souldiers here fetched some old Hedges and Gates to make their Officers and themselves some Fires, else some would have perished in the Cold, being all over a Froth with Sweat in marching. And the old Hedges not being enough, they fetched away the new Ones. The Souldiers had some good Holland's beef in their Snap-sacks which they brought, and their Officers were very glad to get Part with them, so they broil'd it at the Fire. Some had brought Chickens by the way, but raw, which they broil'd and ate, as a most delicate Dish. Sundry Captains offer'd any Mony for a Guide to bring them to a House thereabouts, where they might have some Provisions for their Mony, but no guide could be found, it was exceedingly dark, and being all Strangers, and unacquainted with the country, we could not tell where

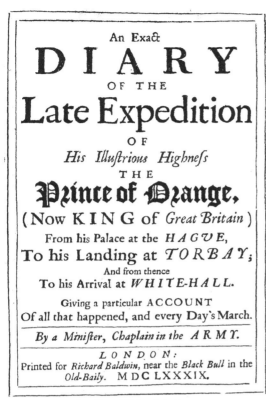

An Exact

D I A R Y

OF THE

Late Expedition

OF

His Illuſtrious Highneſs

THE

𝔓𝔯𝔦𝔫𝔠𝔢 𝔬𝔣 𝔒𝔯𝔞𝔫𝔤𝔢,

(Now **K I N G** of *Great Britain*)

From his Palace at the *H A G V E*,

To his Landing at *T O R B A Y*;

And from thence

To his Arrival at *W H I T E-H A L L.*

Giving a particular A C C O U N T
Of all that happened, and every Day's March.

By a Miniſter, Chaplain in the A R M Y.

L O N D O N:
Printed for *Richard Baldwin*, near the *Black Bull* in the
Old-Baily. M D C LXXXIX.

The Revd Whittle's Diary

to find one House,
for those few that
were scattered here
and there, were either
in some little grove of
Trees, and so hid
from our Eyes, or else
in a bottom amongst
the Hills, and so
could not be seen. We
thought this night al-
most as long as that
in the Storm at Sea,
and judged it to be
Dawn of the Day
some hours before it
was. The Morning ap-
pearing rejoiced at
our very Hearts, for
we thought now we
should march pres-
ently; and we were
sure of this, that
worse Quarters we
could never meet
with, but much better
we hoped to find. A private Souldier going in the next Croft for to
seek a convenient place, he found it to be an Inclosure with Turnips;
so bringing his Burden away with him, he came to the Fire, and gave
those there some, telling his Comrades of the Place, who soon has-
tened there and brought enow with them: Some roasted them, and
others eat them raw, and made a brave Banquet. The Souldiers were
busy in discharging their Musquets, after the Wett and Rain, for they
durst not to trust that Charge: and about 11 of the clock the Army
receiv'd Orders to march. The Place where we encamp'd was trodden
to Dirt, and stuck to our Shoes wretchedly'

At Yalberton at SX8659 5905 stands a cottage with the words 'King
William's Cottage' inscribed above the porch. It is thought that Prince William
rested and took refreshment here before riding on to Longcombe.

At Longcombe in a country lane off the A385 Paignton to Totnes road at
SX8364 5963 is 'Parliament' as marked on the Ordnance Survey maps. It is
likely that it was here that Sir Edward Seymour of Berry Pomeroy met with the
Prince together with other 'Gentlemen of the West' and discussed in council the
future course of the Revolution. A commemorative stone in the garden reads:

WILLIAM
PRINCE OF
ORANGE
IS SAID TO HAVE
HELD HIS FIRST
PARLIAMENT
HERE
IN NOVEMBER
1688

At Newton Abbot the Reverend John Reynel read 'The Declaration' which is commemorated by a stone standing in front of St Leonard's Tower and its inscription reads:

THE FIRST DECLARATION OF
WILLIAM III PRINCE OF ORANGE
THE GLORIOUS DEFENDER OF THE
PROTESTANT RELIGION AND THE
LIBERTIES OF ENGLAND
WAS READ ON THIS PEDESTAL BY
THE REV JOHN REYNEL
RECTOR OF THIS PARISH ON THE
5th NOVEMBER 1688

This lengthy declaration signed and sealed on the 10th October, (an additional second declaration, was written dated 24th October). It basically said that the Prince had been invited by Peers both spiritual and temporal to redress the increasing evils in a Parliament that should be lawfully chosen, and in particular that he would preserve the Church and the established religions. The nearby Wolborough Inn depicts the reading on its Inn sign, but at the time of writing the Inn was in a sorry state and up for sale.

Suspicions were aroused as to the integrity of the claimed birth of a son and heir to the Queen at this time, the latter declaration added:

'to crown all, there was a great and violent presumptions regarding the birth of a son. During the Queen's pretended bigness, and in the manner in which the birth was managed, there were so many just and visible grounds of suspicion that not only himself, but all good subjects vehemently suspected that the pretend child was not born of the Queen'.

In Newton Abbot the bells of the Parish church rang out to welcome the Prince. The Prince stayed at Forde House home of Sir William Courteney where he made his headquarters for a few days and held his first English Council of State. Sir William's son had invited the Prince. Sir William, it was reported was conveniently away at the time, no doubt not to implicate himself should the revolution fail.

(34)
to this place we had an Eaſt and South-Eaſt Wind, which was indeed a good Wind to bring us from *Holland*, and a-long all the Channel, but not to carry us into the Bay, there were ſo many Rocks and Shelves on that ſide. Making ſome Sail again, his Highneſs the Prince of *Orange* gave order that his Standard ſhould be put up ; and accordingly it was done, the White Flag being put up-permoſt, ſignifying his moſt gracious offer of Peace unto all ſuch as would live peaceably : And under that the Red or bloody Flag was ſet up, ſignifying War unto all ſuch as did oppoſe his juſt Deſigns. The Sun recovering ſtrength, ſoon diſſipated the Fog, and diſpers'd the Miſt, infomuch that it prov'd a very pleaſant Day : Now every Veſſel ſet out its Colours, which made a very pleaſant ſhew. By this time the People of *Devonſhire* thereabout had diſco-vered the Fleet, the one telling the other thereof ; they came flocking in droves to the ſide or brow of the Hills to view us : Some gueſs'd we were *French*, becauſe they ſaw divers white Flags ; but the Standard of the Prince, the Motto of which was, **Foʒ the Pʒoteſtant Religion and Libertp,** ſoon undeceived them.

Others more diſcreet ſaid, that it was the *Dutch* Fleet ſo much talk'd of in the Nation, and ſo long expeſted by moſt People. This Day was very remarkable in *England* before, being the fifth of *November*, the Bells were ring-ing as we were ſailing towards the Bay, and as we landed, which many judged to be a good Omen : before we came into the Bays-mouth, as we were near the Rocks, the People ran from Place to Place after us ; and we being ſo near as to ſee and diſcern the Habit of the Country Peo-ple, and they able to ſee us and hear our Voices ; a certain Miniſter in the Fleet, on board the Ship called the *Golden Sun*, went up to the top of the uppermoſt Cabin, where the Colours hang out, a Place where he could eaſily behold all the People on the Shore, and where they might moſt
perfeſtly

Part of the Revd Whittle's diary describing the landing at Torbay

The route: Eastbound

Brixham to HigherYalberton
11.0kms (7.0 miles) Time: 3.0 hrs

From the statue of Prince William of Orange (**Maps 2 & 3**) on the harbour front at Brixham walk round the quayside passing the replica Golden Hind and a commemorative plaque on a stone. It reads 'This plaque was unveiled by Her Majesty the Queen on the 21st July 1988 to commemorate the tercentenary of the landing of Prince William of Orange at Brixham'. Where the road turns sharp left at the Overgang go up the steps on the left keeping to the left of Kelvin Court. At a junction of roads turn sharp right into North Furzeham Rd. Keeping to North Furzeham Rd cross over a road and continue across what greenery is left of Furzeham Common.

Where the road swings left before Battery Gardens go forward into the gardens and turn left. At a cross track continue ahead to exit the gardens to a road. Follow this road round to a dip in the road by Torbay Holiday Chalets and continue up a surfaced footpath ahead marked to 'Churston Ferris'. After 120m where the path turns right around residences turn left through a gate into The Grove. Here turn left on a broad track uphill. Ignoring paths to left and right maintain the main track exiting to a small clearing. Cross the clearing top left to soon enter a field. Cross the centre of the field to exit through a gate, or over a stone stile beside it and onto a broad track, here turn left. Proceed up to a lane in 800m where turn right and in 50m at a T-junction where the main lane turns left continue straight on towards the church.

Follow the lane round past the Church of St Mary the Virgin and along Green Lane and up to a T-junction. Here turn right and in 400m turn left into

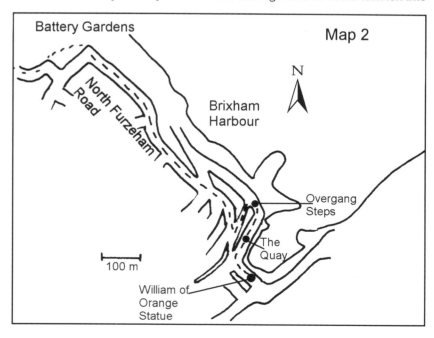

Battery Gardens

Map 2

North Furzeham Road

N

Brixham Harbour

Overgang Steps

The Quay

100 m

William of Orange Statue

Bridge Rd and up to the A3022. Turn right, cross the bridge, and immediately turn down a flight of wooden steps on the right signed 'subway'. Exit the subway up wooden steps on the other side of the A3022 then turn immediately left into Greenway Rd. After 450m at a T-junction turn left and at the Manor Inn fork right on Stoke Gabriel Rd. Exit the village by steep Z bends. After a further 1km at a T-junction in Waddeton at SX 8729 5685 turn right along Waddeton Rd. In 375m at a T-junction turn right and in a further 1.3kms (0.75 miles) at a T-junction turn left along Long Rd passing Yalberton Trading Estates.

In 1.4kms (0.75 miles) at a roundabout continue ahead into Lower Yalberton. At a T-junction at SX8637 5861 turn right along Lower Yalberton Rd and in 500m at a Y-junction turn very sharp left into Yalberton Rd. Immediately on the right is King William's Cottage, Higher Yalberton at SX8659 5905.

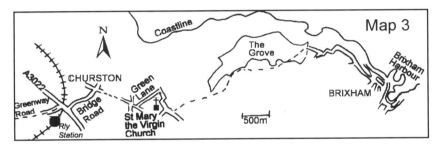

Higher Yalberton to Berry Pomeroy
5.6kms (3.5 miles) Time: 1.5 hrs

From King William's Cottage, Higher Yalberton maintain same direction and follow the lane out of the village to a T-junction where turn left. In 600m at Whitehill, at SX8574 5880 branch right up Coombe House Lane. After 1.2kms (0.75 miles) reach a lane (Lembury Rd) at a T-junction where turn right and in a further 1.5kms (1.0 miles) pass by 'Parliament' at Longcombe at SX8364 5963 (*a residence where Prince William held his first Council Meeting, a commemorative stone is outside*) and on up to the A385 at Longcombe Cross. Cross over the road and go down a lane passing in front of cottages to a T-junction where turn right. After 1.0kms arrive at a T-junction in Berry Pomeroy, turn left and walk up to the Parish Church of St Mary, Berry Pomeroy.

Berry Pomeroy to Ipplepen
9.0kms (5.5 miles) Time: 3.0 hrs

Special note: In wet weather some bridleways on this leg can be muddy, or flooded, it may be advisable to walk in wellies. As in William's day the mud 'stuck to our shoes wretchedly'.

From the Parish Church of St Mary, Berry Pomeroy walk back 100m to the previously mentioned T-junction, follow the road round to the left and in 100m turn right on a path leading up to a gate. Go through the gate and into a field to proceed on the left-hand side up the field to exit at the top left through a gate and to a lane. Cross over the lane and immediately at a

Parliament, Longcombe

Photo: A Hart

Y-junction take the left fork marked 'Berry Pomeroy Castle' and 'Afton'. After 400m at Berry Castle Lodge turn left over a metal bar stile and enter the castle grounds along a driveway. In 250m after a gate take the footpath on the right leading uphill.

Soon good views of Berry Pomeroy Castle are seen below. *Berry Pomeroy Castle is owned by His Grace the Duke of Somerset and is in the care of English Heritage.* At the end of the path turn left to walk back towards the castle. Just before the castle turn right down a path into the valley exiting through a gate to a lane. Maintain the same direction up to a T-junction in 100m. Here turn left and in 150m at Afton Bridge turn right along a lane. After 600m just after where the lane turns left, turn right on a bridleway to pass a residence and join another bridleway and on ahead. In 200m cross over a ford and continue on the main bridleway uphill ignoring a footpath on the right. Follow this bridleway for 800m up to a lane (Smallwell Lane).

Cross over the lane and continue on the path ahead to pass behind farm buildings and to a cross track. Proceed on the path opposite marked 'Aptor Lane' and in 1km reach a lane (Ipplepen Rd). Here turn left and in 300m at 'Windthorn' turn left along a bridleway. After 400m at a cross track continue on along the bridleway (Wrigwell Lane) and after 1km cross over a railway bridge at Wrigwell and walk on ahead, now on a surfaced lane. In 800m walk up to a T-junction where turn left and in 30m go up to the A381 at Wrigwell Cross. Here turn right and walk along the A381 for 150m (*taking care*) then turn left along Clampitt Rd. In 300m turn right down Croft Rd and walk up to a crossroads at East St/Dornafield Rd in Ipplepen.

Ipplepen to Abbotskerwell
4.0kms (2.5 miles) Time: 1.0 hrs

Special note: In wet weather some bridleways on this leg can be muddy, or flooded, it may be advisable to walk in wellies.

From the crossroads of Croft Rd East St and Dornafield Rd go forward along Dornafield Rd for 400m then turn right over a metal bar stile to a footpath. In 150m exit over a metal bar stile to a lane where turn left and in 20m turn right over a stile by a gate into Clannon Farm. Just after a Y-junction to a residence go left down steps to follow a stream. Then go through two kissing gates and on into Fermoy's Nursery. Turn left and pass by greenhouses on your right and follow the path round the nursery and into their car park. Walk ahead through the car park exiting at the top left-hand corner to the A381.

Cross over the road and turn left along it walking on the grass verge (*taking care*) for 400m to Two Mile Oak Cross. Turn right into Whiddon Rd and in 700m turn left down a bridleway and in 150m turn right over a stile to cross a field on bearing about 40 degrees. Exit over a double stile in a hedgerow and on across another field to join the corner of a wood where turn left and then walk alongside a stone wall. Exit over a stile by farm buildings and proceed up to the end of a lane by RNID buildings.

Here turn right and go down a track to the left of the entrance to the RNID and descend to exit into Grange Rd. Go forward to cross a road and down a short path by the Court Farm Inn. Then turn right through a gate to go round to the left and up to a T-junction where turn left and walk up to a T-junction in Abbotskerwell by the post office.

Abbotskerwell to Newton Abbot
4.0kms (2.5 miles) Time: 1.25 hrs

From the T-junction by the post office in Abbotskerwell walk along Slade Lane and in 200m turn right up Ford Rd (Map 4)to a crossroads at Manor Rd. Cross over the road and go up Laburnum Terrace. At its end go forward between residences and over a stile into a field. Go uphill across the field to pass to the left of three trees and exit over a stile by a gate to a lane. Turn left along the lane for 80m and then turn right over a stile and into a field. Walk up the field alongside the hedgerow and at the end of the hedgerow continue on in the same direction to a beacon on top of the hill at SX8578 6952.

Bear left over the hill and walk down the hill on bearing 40 degrees aiming for the left corner of a wood (Decoy Brake). Cross over a stile and enter a field, keeping to the right-hand side descend the field alongside the wood to exit in the bottom right-hand corner and into Decoy Country Park. In 30m cross a track and walk on ahead. In 100m at a Y-junction take the left fork. At a T-junction on a bend turn left then later join the end of a broad track by a gate. Here turn right and walk up to a perimeter track round a lake (*formerly a quarry which is 165 feet deep*). Turn right and follow the track round the lake to arrive at the Ranger's Office area where turn right to go through a car park.

Turn left to exit the main gates to a road (Decoy Rd). Here turn left and in 400m turn right into Forde Park and go down the hill to cross a junction and into

Courtlands Rd, at its end join Station Rd and go forward to cross the pedestrian crossing in front of the railway station in Newton Abbot.

The route: Westbound

Newton Abbot to Abbotskerwell
4.0kms (2.5 miles) Time: 1.25 hrs

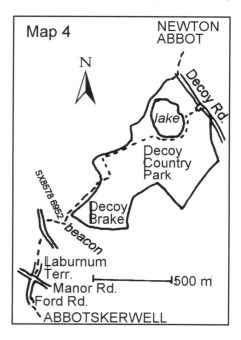

Map 4   NEWTON ABBOT   N

From Newton Abbot railway station cross over the pedestrian crossing in front of the station and turn left along Station Rd. At a Y-junction take the right fork into Courtlands Rd. In 100m cross over a crossroads and go ahead into Forde Park (Map 4). Just over the top of the hill turn left into Decoy Rd and in 400m turn right into Decoy Country Park. Turn right through a car park passing the Ranger's Office and up to the lake. Turn left and follow the main path round the lake to the opposite side where turn left over a footbridge on a broad footpath on bearing 240 degrees. At the end of the path and before a gate turn left over another footbridge. At a T-junction turn right, and go straight on to cross a track by a gate and in 30m go over a stile and into a field. Walk up the field on the left-hand side alongside Decoy Brake. Exit the field in the top left-hand corner over a stile and into a hilly field. Leaving the wooded area go forward up to the beacon at SX8578 6952 on bearing about 220 degrees.

Leave the beacon on bearing about 290 degrees and then walk alongside a hedgerow on the left to the corner of the field exiting over a stile to a lane. Here turn left and in 80m turn right over a stile into a field. Go down the field passing to the right of three trees and then exit over a stile between residences. Continue ahead to walk down Laburnum Terrace to a crossroads at Manor Rd. Go forward down Ford Rd and at its end turn left along Slade Lane. In 200m arrive at a T-junction by the post office in Abbotskerwell.

Abbotskerwell to Ipplepen
4.0kms (2.5 miles) Time: 1.0 hrs

Special note: In wet weather some bridleways on this leg can be muddy, or flooded, it may be advisable to walk in wellies.

From the T-junction by the post office in Abbotskerwell walk in a southerly direction for 80m and then turn right down a lane by the Church House. In a further 70m turn left on a footpath up to Court Farm Inn. Go through a gate and take the short footpath leading left up to a road. Cross over the road and go up Grange Rd and in 20m turn right up a footpath by residences. At the top exit by an entrance to RNID buildings.

Go past the entrance and turn left up a short driveway to a farm and cross over a stile into a field. Walk alongside a stone wall and then a hedgerow and at its end go half-right on bearing about 220 degrees to exit over a double stile in a hedgerow into another field. Cross the field maintaining direction to exit over a stile to a bridleway, here turn left and in 150m walk up to a lane (Whiddon Rd). Turn right and in 700m reach the A381 at Two Mile Oak Cross.

Here turn left and walk along the grass verge *(taking care)* and in 400m at Fermoy's Nursery turn right through their car park. Keep to the right-hand edge and go forward onto a path to skirt left round the edge of the nursery. After passing greenhouses exit in the bottom right-hand corner to a path. Go through two kissing gates and alongside a stream then up steps to a driveway. Follow the driveway to exit over a stile to a lane, here turn left and in 20m turn right over a metal bar stile. In 150m exit over a metal bar stile to a lane (Dornafield Rd). Here turn left and in 400m up to a crossroads at East St in Ipplepen.

Ipplepen to Berry Pomeroy
9.0kms (5.5 miles) Time: 3.0 hrs

Special note: In wet weather some bridleways on this leg can be muddy, or flooded, it may be advisable to walk in wellies.

From the crossroads East St/Dornafield Rd and Croft Rd walk down Croft Rd to a T-junction with Clampitt Rd. Turn left and walk up to the A381. Here turn right and in 150m *(taking care)* at Wrigwell Cross turn left down a lane marked 'Wrigwell' and 'Dainton'. In 30m turn right along a lane marked 'Wrigwell' (a quarter of a mile). After 800m cross over a railway bridge where the lane becomes unsurfaced (Wrigwell Lane) and in a further 1km at a cross track maintain direction for another 400m up to a lane (Ipplepen Rd) at 'Windthorn'. Turn right and in 300m turn right up a bridleway marked 'Aptor Lane'.

After 1km go forward over a cross track to descend round farm buildings at Aptor and down to a lane (Smallwell Lane). Cross the lane and proceed on the bridleway opposite for 1km and to a lane. Here turn left and in 600m reach a T-junction at Afton Bridge. Turn left and in 150m turn right along a lane. In 100m go left through a gate into the wooded grounds of Berry Pomeroy Castle. *Berry Pomeroy Castle is owned by His Grace the Duke of Somerset and is in the care of English Heritage.* At the top of the path is the castle, here turn left away from the car park and castle and in 60m turn sharp right to gain a path leading to a higher level back past the castle.

Berry Pomeroy Castle

Photo: A Hart

The path descends to join a driveway through a gate, follow the driveway to exit from the grounds over a metal bar stile by Berry Castle Lodge and up to a lane. Here turn right and in 400m at a Y-junction cross over the road and go into a field by a gate on the left. Walk down the field aiming for the church on bearing about 230 degrees to exit in the bottom right-hand corner through a gate and up to a road. Turn left and in 100m at a T-junction turn right and walk up to the Parish Church of St Mary, Berry Pomeroy.

Berry Pomeroy to Higher Yalberton
5.6kms (3.5 miles) Time: 1.5 hrs

From the Parish Church of St Mary, Berry Pomeroy walk in an easterly direction back to the previously mentioned T-junction in 100m, here turn right. In about 1km and just before the A385 take a left fork to pass by cottages and up to the A385 at Longcombe Cross. Cross over the road and go down the lane opposite. In 600m pass by 'Parliament' at Longcombe at SX8364 5963 (*a residence where Prince William held his first Council Meeting, a commemorative stone is outside*).

Proceed on past 'Parliament' and in 600m after passing through Aish along Lembury Rd, turn left at a T-junction (Coombe House Cross) at SX8459 5873 along Coombe House Lane. In 1.2kms (0.75 miles) at a Y-junction at Whitehill SX8574 5880 maintain direction along Stoke Rd. In 600m at a T-junction SX8625 5960 turn right into Higher Yalberton and in 400m up to a cottage on the left just short of a Y-junction, (King William's Cottage) at SX8659 5905.

Higher Yalberton to Brixham
11.0kms (7.0 miles) Time: 3.0 hrs

From the above mentioned cottage go up to the Y-junction and turn very sharp right into Lower Yalberton Rd and after 500m up to a T-junction in Lower Yalberton. Here turn left and soon continue on across a roundabout then pass a trading estate on Long Rd. After 1.5kms (1.0 miles) up to a T-junction where turn right into Waddeton Rd. In 1.3kms (0.75 miles) at a Y-junction bear left into Waddeton. At a T-junction turn left along Stoke Gabriel Rd. Follow this road to its terminal point to arrive at the Manor Inn at Galmpton at a Y-junction.

At the Y-junction proceed on in the same direction along Greenway Rd to soon bear right, maintaining Greenway Rd (Map 3) and in 500m just before the A3022 go down a flight of wooden steps on the right signed 'subway'. Exit the subway on the other side of the A3022 up wooden steps and immediately turn left over the bridge and left into Bridge Rd. At its end turn right and in 400m turn left along Green Lane. At its end turn right and follow the road round past the Church of St Mary the Virgin, Churston Ferris. Follow the road which then swings left away from the church and Churston Court and proceed to a T-junction. Go forward in the same direction for 50m then turn left along a track marked 'To The Grove'.

After 800m where the track goes left into The Grove turn right through a gate, or over a stone stile beside it and across the centre of a field. Exit in the top right-hand corner onto a broad track. Continue on ahead to a small open space exiting on the left fork into a wooded area (part of The Grove) and downhill. At a point where the path swings left, turn right through a gate and onto a narrow surfaced path behind residences. In a further 130m go down to a road by Torbay Holiday Chalets.

Continue on the road ahead for 100m and enter Battery Gardens (Map 2) at a point where the road turns right. At a cross track continue on exiting the gardens in the top right-hand corner and into North Furzeham Rd. Proceed along this road to cross what is left of the greenery of Furzeham common. At a road junction go forward keeping to North Furzeham Rd bearing left after 30m. At a junction of roads, Overgang/Higher St/Prospect Rd, turn very sharp left down Overgang. Go forward to descend steps to the harbour. At the bottom of the steps turn right and go round the quayside and up to the statue of Prince William of Orange at Brixham.

Commemorative stone at Parliament, Longcombe

Photo: A Hart

Newton Abbot to Exeter

Map: OS Explorer 110,114
Start: Railway Station Newton Abbot
Finish: Exeter Cathedral
Distance: 38.0 kms (23.5 miles)
Time: 9.5 hrs
Transport: Railway: Newton Abbot, Exeter
                  Buses: Newton Abbot, Kingsteignton, Chudleigh, Shillingford
St George (Infrequent), Exminster, Exeter
Place of historical interest: Commemorative stone St Leonard's Tower
Newton Abbot, Forde House Newton Abbot, Ugbrooke House Chudleigh,
Chudleigh Rocks and Caves, West Gate Exeter, The Cathedral and Deanery
Exeter

The History

After Newton Abbot, the Revd Whittle describes the army passing by a 'Popish Lady's House' which has been suggested that this was the wife of Thomas, Baron Clifford owner of Ugbrooke and lies about 1.5kms (1 mile) south east from Chudleigh. Prince William ordered that it should be left unmolested.

In Chudleigh the Prince had his headquarters at Cholwichs, a house in the town centre, which has since been destroyed by fire. It was then owned by the Poulett family and lived in by the Reverend John Gawler and his wife Bridget. When King James's forces occupied the town Reverend Gawler, a Protestant had to hide in the nearby caves (Chudleigh Rocks) until the arrival of William's army.

Later the Prince crossed Haldon Hill and on through Shillingford St George and across the River Exe and then by way of the West Gate to a great welcome by the city dignitaries in the streets of Exeter.

Once in Exeter Prince William was to lodge at the Cathedral Deanery for about twelve days. His troops were still billeted in the villages along the road from Newton Abbot and eventually arrived to a well-earned rest from the grueling journey through the red mud of Devon made worse by the heavy rains. Whilst in Exeter Prince William was able to attend to his concerns regarding payment to his army and the purchase of their day to day food and fodder for his horses. With his hands on the local tax machine and the recruitment of eminent Englishmen to administer it, he ensured both their loyalties to him, and implicating them in ensuring the revolutions success, at their expense of answering to the King about their actions should it fail. Supplies bound for the English naval base at Plymouth were seized by William and put to his own use. All along the route Prince William had insisted upon the good behaviour of his troops and in Exeter, the Revd Whittle commented that:

'when we were there, the city was more quiet in the Night and freer from Debauch'd and disorderly persons than 'twas before'. The local populous was amazed at the make-up of William's army. There were fair-haired men from Scandinavia, black men from the sugar

plantations, Africans in strange headgear and Swedish horsemen in armour and fur cloaks'.

The Prince attended a Cathedral service to give thanks for his safe arrival. William's stay in Exeter allowed him to recruit locally and for his army to refresh itself. During his time in Exeter sympathetic uprisings by his supporters gained Derby on the 17th November and Nottingham on the 20th.

A great part of William's heavy and bulky ordnance was to come ashore at Topsham thus avoiding some of those difficulties experienced by the army on their march from Brixham. It was then taken to Exeter to join the army in their first headquarters.

It was in Exeter that we first encounter the double agent Hugh Speke, a Protestant. In later years Speke was to write an account of events in 1688 and in particular of his own involvement.

Speke tells us:

'The King told him that he was to go over to the Prince of Orange, and insinuate himself into his Camp, and to give him a particular Account of the Prince's Strength, Motions and Designs'.

Money and some blank passes were given to Speke to achieve this spying mission. After being held overnight along the way by the King's troops to verify his pass he was allowed to continue to Exeter. Upon arrival in Exeter he had an audience with William, Speke revealed his true mission to William and offered the blank passes for his officers to use as they saw fit.

Speke continues on:

'Speke at the same time kept up a constant correspondence with the King and sent him an Account of the Princes's Army according to his Promise, but always made it three times larger than it was'.

Commemorative stone at St Leonard's Tower, Newton Abbott

Photo: A Hart

The route: Eastbound

Newton Abbot to Chudleigh
12.5 kms (7.75 miles) Time 3.0 hrs.

From Newton Abbot railway station walk towards the town centre along Queen St. Turn right into The Avenue and at a roundabout turn right to cross a bridge and then turn immediately left along a path marked 'Templer Way'. Continue on this well-defined gravel path and alongside the disused Stover Canal first left over the canal and then into a clearing exiting Jetty Marsh Local Nature Reserve. At a concrete sluice construction over the main body of the canal turn right soon to go through a gate and going on ahead. Keep on ahead into a wooded area (Map 5) and at a road (Exeter Rd) turn right to cross a single-track railway and a stone bridge to regain the Templer Way on the opposite bank of the Stover Canal.

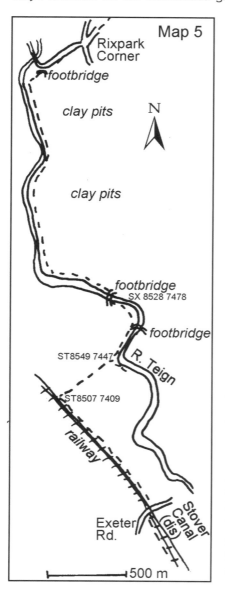

Proceed on ahead to cross a plank bridge, two stiles then a kissing gate and ahead with fields on your right. Cross two more plank bridges and past a sad looking lock. At a kissing gate enter a field and in a few paces walk up to a finger post at SX8507 7409 marked 'Templer Way Heritage Trail, Stover via Ventiford'. Here turn right and cross the field then crossing another plank bridge and kissing gate and across another field. Go through a kissing gate in a hedgerow and across another field and in 50m up to a finger post by the River Teign at SX8594 7447. Here turn left and follow the riverside path into another field, passing a footbridge on the right (do not cross) exiting through a hedgerow into another field.

In 30m cross the footbridge on the right at SX8528 7478 over the River Teign then turn left and follow the course of the river across a field. Then leaving the field through a gate go into a wooded area. Follow this path alongside the river with unseen clay pits on your right. At a

T-junction of paths in 1.2kms (0.75 miles) turn right (marked on a tree by the river) and in 150m up to a road. Here turn right along the road and walk along the grass verge on the left-hand side of the road (*taking great care*) and in 300m up to a crossroads (Rixpark Corner signed Rixypark). Cross the junction and on ahead up a lane and in 1.3kms (0.75 miles) up to a junction of roads.

Here turn left and after 150m where the lane turns right take the footpath on the left, go over a stile and into a field. Follow the hedgerow then aiming for a point halfway down the side of the hill on bearing about 20 degrees, walk towards a stile on the far side of the field in a hedgerow. Cross the stile and cross the field maintaining height to a point right of a tree line. Go round this tree line and turn left into the neck of the field heading downhill by the side of a lane and go into a wooded area. Exit over a stile and go into a field keeping to the right to exit over a second stile on the right in 20m to a lane. Here turn left and in 10m at a bend in the lane turn right along a track on bearing about 30 degrees ignoring the path to the right.

Follow this right of way track towards Lawell House following the line of evenly spaced trees. Where the path bears left downhill follow it alongside Lawell House wall, to cross a stream at a footbridge. After 20m go left through a gate and uphill soon exiting through another gate to walk up the left-hand side of a field to exit through a gate at a road, the B3344 at SX8620 7875. (*To your right are Chudleigh Rocks and Caves where the Reverend John Gawler, a Protestant, hid whilst avoiding King James' troops.*) Here turn right along the road and in just over 1km arrive at the War Memorial and crossroads in Chudleigh along Fore St.

Chudleigh to Shillingford St George
10.5kms (6.5 miles) Time: 2.5 hrs

From the war memorial in Chudleigh walk north along Old Exeter St later Old Exeter Road. At Milestone Cross continue ahead for 3.5kms (2.25 miles) ignoring other roads to arrive at an angled crossroads at Buller Cross at SX8856 8473. Maintaining the same direction leave this crossroads by the road diagonally opposite marked 'Clapham'. Keep to this road for a further 2.8kms (1.75 miles) to Clapham. At a T-junction turn left, and in 100m, turn sharp right to Shillingford St George. In 1.2kms (0.75 miles) on entering Shillingford St George turn right on a footpath opposite St George Terrace to walk up to St George's Church.

Shillingford St George to Exminster
5.5kms (3.5 miles) Time: 1.5 hrs

From St George's Church in Shillingford St George walk through the car park to a lane where turn left. In 150m at a T-junction turn right. At a stream the lane becomes unsurfaced and goes uphill. At the summit where the lane bends right turn left through a gate and into a field, soon catching sight of the River Exe in the distance. Walk along the right-hand edge of the field for 800m exiting through a gate to a lane. Walk down the lane and in 200m cross over the A379 and on ahead on the lane opposite, Days-Pottles Lane. In 900m cross overhead the A38(T) road, and in a further 2.1kms (1.25 miles) up to a T-junction in Exminster. Here turn right and in 700m down to a roundabout on the A379.

Exminster to Exeter
9.5kms (6.0 miles) Time: 2.5 hrs

From the roundabout on the A379 at Exminster walk east along a lane towards the River Exe passing the disused Exminster railway station. Cross over the railway bridge and on ahead, the lane becomes a track later. At a car park and ferry point in just over 1km from the railway bridge join the Exeter Canal towpath. Here turn left and follow the towpath and after 1.2kms (0.75 miles) go underneath the M5 motorway. In a further 1.6kms (1.0 mile) go up to Countess Wear Swing Bridge. Cross over the road and continue ahead on the towpath for almost 3.0km (2.0 miles) to the terminal point of the canal where it joins the River Exe, having passed the Welcome Inn on the left.

Turn right over a swing bridge by a lock and continue on ahead alongside the River Exe. In 800m go up to a road bridge over the river. Here turn left up a path to the road level and immediately right crossing Exeter Bridge South. Cross over the road into Edmund St and then turn right to cross the West Gate ruins (*William would have entered the city this way*). Exiting the West Gate ruins continue on ahead into West St on the left passing the Old House (that was moved, note nearby plaque on the wall to William's entry into Exeter) on the left. Cross over West St and go up Stepcote Hill (*beside St Mary Steps Church with Matthew Miller clock*) then ahead into Smythen St. At a T-junction with Market St turn left and soon reach Fore St. Here turn right and at a crossroads of Fore St, High St, North St and South St go half-right through a covered entranceway and into the area of Exeter Cathedral and on up to the Cathedral.

The route: Westbound

Exeter to Exminster
9.5kms (6.0 miles) Time: 2.5 hrs

From the main doors of the Exeter Cathedral walk towards the monument (War Memorial) and go through a covered entranceway into South St. Cross over the road half-right and continue along Fore St to the next junction. Turn left into Market St and then right into Smythen St, then ahead down steep Stepcote Hill and across West St. Pass by the Old House (*that was moved: note nearby plaque on the wall to William's entry into Exeter*). Continue ahead to the West Gate ruins. Cross the ruins and then turn left along Edmund St. Cross over the road and turn right to cross Exeter Bridge South and then turn left down steps to the river and then right along the riverside, the river on your left. After 800m cross over the right-hand swing bridge to walk along the right hand side of the Exeter Canal from its originating point, soon passing the Welcome Inn. In less than 3.0km (2.0 miles) go up to the Countess Wear Swing Bridge. Cross the road and continue on the canal towpath ahead marked 'Turf Locks Hotel 3 miles'. After 1.6kms (1.0 miles) pass under the M5 motorway and in a further 1.2kms (0.75 miles) go up to a car park and ferry point. Here turn right, away from the canal along a track that becomes a lane. In just over 1km cross a bridge by the disused Exminster railway station and on up to a road junction, the A379, at a roundabout at Exminster.

Exminster to Shillingford St. George
5.5kms (3.5 miles) Time: 1.5 hrs

From the roundabout on the A379 at Exminster take the road into Exminster and over a second roundabout by the Royal Oak. In a further 500m turn left along Days-Pottles Lane. Follow this lane for 2.1kms (1.25 miles) to cross overhead the A38 (T) road and in a further 900m up to a T-junction with the A379. Cross this road and go up the bridleway opposite.

In 200m at three gates, go through the small gate next to the right hand gate and into a field. Continuing in the same direction alongside the left hedgerow. After 800m exit through a gate to a lane and cross track. Here turn right and go downhill maintaining the main track and onto a surfaced lane. At a T-junction where the lane turns right, turn left and in 150m turn right through a small car park and into the grounds of the village church of St George's at Shillingford St George.

Shillingford St George to Chudleigh
10.5kms (6.5 miles) Time: 2.5 hrs

From the village church of St George's in Shillingford St George walk in a northerly direction for a 100m to a lane opposite St George Terrace. Here turn left along the lane. Follow this lane for 1.2kms (0.75 miles) to Clapham turning sharp left to arrive at a T-junction in a further 150m. Here turn right on a lane to Chudleigh and in a further 2.8kms (1.75 miles) to arrive at an angled crossroads at Buller Cross at SX8856 8473.

Cross the road maintaining direction on a lane diagonally opposite, to Chudleigh. In a further 3.5kms (2.25 miles) along Old Exeter Rd arrive at Milestone Cross. Continue ahead into Chudleigh in a further 1.7kms (1.0 miles) to arrive in Chudleigh along Old Exeter St and up to the war memorial at a crossroads.

Chudleigh to Newton Abbot
12.5 kms (7.75 miles) Time: 3.0 hrs

From the War Memorial crossroads in Chudleigh walk south along Fore St passing the church and after about 1km turn left through a gate on a public right of way at SX8620 7875. Walk down the right-hand side of the field to go through a gate and downhill to exit another gate where turn right. (*To your left are Chudleigh Rocks and Caves where the Reverend John Gawler, a Protestant, hid whilst avoiding King James's troops*). Continue on to cross a footbridge over a stream and then uphill alongside the wall of Lawell House. At a junction of paths bear right to follow a line of evenly spaced trees, then go through a gate eventually exiting to a lane on a bend

Here turn left and in 10m turn right over a stile into a field. Turn left and in 20m turn left again over a stile into a wooded area. Exit over a stile into the narrow neck of a field. Keep to the right-hand edge of the wooded area and at its end continue across a sloping field on bearing about 180 degrees to exit over a stile in a hedgerow. Cross the stile into another sloping field and continue on in the same direction aiming for the point of a hedgerow. Then follow the hedgerow up to the top right-hand corner to exit the field over a stile to a lane on a bend. Here turn right and in 150m at a junction of lanes turn right down a lane before a cottage.

After 1.3kms (0.75 miles) at a crossroads (Rixpark Corner, signed Rixypark) (Map 5) continue on the road opposite marked 'Heathfield' and 'Bovey Tracey'. Walk along the grass verge on the right-hand side of the road (*taking great care*) for 300m and where the road swings right, turn left down a footpath, over a footbridge and up to the River Teign. Here turn left and walk alongside the river for 1.2kms (0.75 miles) with unseen clay pits on the left, then exit through a gate to a field. Continue on following the riverside path for a further 600m to cross over a footbridge on the right at SX8528 7478 over the River Teign. Here turn left and in 30m go through a gap into another field to proceed along the riverside to pass another footbridge in 300m (do not cross) and on into another field.

At a bend in the river before the end of the field, at a finger post at SX8594 7447, turn right following the Templer Way footpath Heritage Trail. After 50m go through a kissing gate in a hedgerow and into another field. At another hedgerow go through another kissing gate and across a plank bridge over a ditch and across a field and up to a finger post at SX8507 7409. Here turn left towards Teignbridge Crossing and immediately go through a kissing gate. Continue on ahead alongside the disused Stover Canal on your right. At a kissing gate enter a small wooded area and over two stiles and a plank bridge.

Then onto a gravelled path and up to a road (Exeter Rd) by a stone bridge. Here turn right and cross the bridge and then a single-track railway, turning left immediately before the second stone bridge. Take the right-hand path into a wooded area and through a chicane over a stream and continue on a well-defined path. Go through a gate and on ahead up to a second gate. Here turn left over a concrete bridge into a wooded area (Jetty Marsh Local Nature Reserve). Then walking past Templer Way Jetty Marsh Canal Basin continue ahead and up to a road. Here turn right and cross over the bridge and up to a roundabout. Turn left into The Avenue and up to Queen St where turn left and walk round to Newton Abbot railway station.

Exeter to Honiton

Map: OS Explorer 114, 115
Start: Exeter Cathedral
Finish: New St/High St Honiton
Distance: 45.3kms (28.25 miles)
Time: 11.75 hrs
Transport: Railway: Exeter, Topsham, Honiton
                Buses: Exeter, Topsham, (Woodbury, Tipton St John,
infrequently), Newton Poppleford (500m south of Harpford Bridge), Ottery St
Mary, Honiton
Place of historical interest: West Gate Exeter, The Cathedral and Deanery
Exeter, Quayside Topsham, Escot House home of Sir Walter Yonge

See Special Note on page 40 regarding Exeter to Topsham

The West Gate, Exeter

Photo: L Ham

The history

Topsham was the place where Prince William chose to bring ashore his heavy ordnance and had special unloading equipment brought from Holland for the task. It was then taken to Exeter to join the main body of William's army. In the Register of Deaths in the Parish Records of Topsham there are contained entries of four persons, notably Sir William Hamilton (recorded as Hambleton), who was Prince William's Master of Ordnance buried on the 8th December 1688. Others were 'a Dutch Soldyer' buried on the 11th November 1688, 'a Lieutenant' buried on the 5th December 1688 and 'a Soldyer' buried on the 19th December 1688, noted in the records as probably in the retinue of Sir William Hambleton.

It wasn't until after William's army had passed through Exeter that they were in better shape. One man after Exeter was worth two before was the word. Sir Walter Yonge of Escot House near Ottery St Mary was the first to commit his local militia to William's cause and subsequently arranged to provide accommodation for William's troops. Once William's troops were ensconced in Ottery St Mary he reviewed them.

Lord Cornbury a Colonel of the Royal Dragoons deserted the King with 200 troops and horses and joined William at Honiton. Cornbury's defection heralded others to follow and support the rebel cause.

Plaque at West Gate, Exeter

Photo: L Ham

The route: Eastbound

Exeter to Topsham
8.0kms (5.0 miles) Time: 2.0 hrs

Special Note: Although walking part of this leg is possible at low tides, it remains wet and slippery and might be a problem to those walkers carrying heavy backpacks. On this leg it is NOT advisable to walk it at high tide or when the River Exe is in flood. An alternative route round a 1.4km section is advised, see page 41.

From the main doors of Exeter Cathedral walk towards the monument (War Memorial) and go through a covered entranceway into South St. Cross over the road half-right and continue along Fore St to the next junction. Turn left into Market St and then right into Smythen St then ahead down steep Stepcote Hill and across West St. Pass by the Old House on the right (*that was moved, note nearby plaque on wall to William's entry into Exeter*). Continue ahead to the West Gate ruins. Walk past the original West Gate and over the arches, exiting near two bridges over the River Exe. Turn left and go down a subway exiting to St Thomas's. Then immediately turn left alongside the River Exe, the river on your right. After 250m and passing a pedestrian footbridge to the other bank, continue ahead over a footbridge maintaining the left bank. Walk past ferry points and on through a metal gate after 400m.

In a further 500m at a footbridge proceed ahead. Cross a road and regain the riverside after 450m. Cross a road between Salmonpool Lane and Old Abbey Court continuing on behind dwellings. Ignoring a footbridge, take the path marked 'Burnthouse Lane' through a wooded area. The path swings sharp left then right and amongst dwellings. Walk on ahead on a footpath behind St Loye's College. At a T-junction of paths turn left and almost immediately right up to the Crematorium Rd. Cross over the road and continue on a tree-lined path with a golf course on the left. Immediately after crossing a bridge over a stream turn right, to walk round the edge of the golf course exiting through a kissing gate in a wooded area. Turn left passing Countess Wear Paper Mills (1638-1885) along Mill Lane. At a road (Mill Rd) turn right which then becomes a surfaced path. At Countess Wear Rd turn right, passing Mount Wear House (YHA) and the Countess Wear House built in 1715 with Bell Tower and Weather Vane, and up to the A379.

Cross over the A379 and continue ahead on Glasshouse Lane. Ignoring Lower Wear Rd go ahead down a lane and just after where the road swings sharp left take the public footpath on the right marked 'Topsham'. Cross over stile and ahead to a metal gate and then down some steps. (**At this point take the detour route (below) if it is wet, high tide or the River Exe is in flood**) Here turn right and after 30m turn left through thick vegetation eventually emerging by a wall and residences. Continue along the riverside ledge footpath and under the M5 Bridge passing the Retreat Boatyard and up to Topsham Playing Fields at Ashford Rd and Ferry Rd. (**Detour re-joins here**) Proceed on the road ahead Ferry Rd passing Follet Rd, and Passage House Inn. Continue past Exe St and along Strand, just before a road junction turn right into the quayside area at Topsham.

Detour route: After descending the steps turn left through a gate then turn right on a footpath to walk behind houses and up to a road (Topsham Rd). Here turn right and follow the road, which becomes Exeter Rd under the M5 motorway and after a further 700m turn right down Ashford Rd. In 200m at a bend rejoin the path at the exit point from Topsham Playing Fields turning left along Ferry Rd. **End of detour** (Go back to last paragraph).

Topsham to Woodbury
7.1kms (4.5 miles) Time: 1.75 hrs

From Topsham quayside walk past the Lighter Inn and cross over the road into Holman Way. After 400m turn right through a gate by the railway track. Cross over the active railway line (*take care*) and ahead on a path at a road turn right. Follow the main road down the hill to cross over the River Clyst. In 600m, and after a left-hand bend take a footpath on the right by a stream. In 300m after passing between houses at a junction, turn left along a surfaced lane. At a road (A376) cross over it and go up Old Ebford Lane opposite and into Ebford village. In 200m turn left into Lower Lane. After 500m at a T-junction turn right and in 800m after a sharp right, turn left and up to a road the B3179. Cross over the B3179 and turn right and in 30m turn left up a lane towards Postlake Farm. After 250m where the road swings right and left, turn sharp right onto a farm track, Moor Lane.

The farm track becomes a path then a farm track again and after 1.2kms (0.75 mile) where the track joins a lane on a bend near Pilehayes Farm, turn right over a stile into a field. Keep to left-hand edge of field and in 200m turn left to follow the hedgerow to a lane (Bond's Lane). Turn right and in 200m just after 'Buckfield' turn left on track. After 5m cross over a stile and enter a field on the right. Turn left and follow the hedgerow on the left. After 300m cross over a stile and into a field exiting at a metal gate after 500m by Woodbury Centenary allotments and to a lane at a T-junction. Turn left down the lane (Pound Lane) and follow it round to a road at Parsonage Cross in Woodbury.

Woodbury to Harpford Bridge
11.5kms (7.25 miles) Time: 3.25 hrs

From the Parsonage Cross after exiting Pound Lane in Woodbury turn left along a road and in 200m turn right into Cottles Lane (**Map 6**). The lane joins a road after 700m here turn left and in 100m turn right through a gate onto a bridleway between hedgerows at Cottles Farm. Go through a second gate and turn left keeping to the left-hand side of the field. Continue ahead through a gate into another field and down a hill exiting through a gate and into a wood. Go forward ignoring paths to left and right on compass bearing 120 degrees and after 300m emerging to walk along the edge of Rushmoor Wood, then ahead up a track to join the 'East Devon Way' at SY0305 8732. Here turn left up a broad path through a wood.

After 500m, at a road, turn right and in 400m go up to the B3180 at a T-junction. Cross over the B3180 and take the footpath opposite. After 200m take the right-hand fork to join a path coming up from the right. Proceed on bearing 90 degrees passing the site of Woodbury Castle Fort on the right and on ahead over Colaton Raleigh Common in an overall general direction of about 70 degrees keeping to the left of the military danger area and ignoring paths to left or right.

At a copse and cross track at SY0423 8800 maintain the same direction. After 50m take the left fork on bearing 80 degrees and ignoring all cross tracks eventually descending to the road junction at Hawkerland at SY0602 8865. Here turn left and after 100m turn right up a lane at a T-junction. After 200m take the track leading off to the left. Keep to the broad track ignoring paths to left and right in the general direction of 340 degrees.

After 700m at a cross track turn right before the wood (**Map 7**), and up to a road. Turn left passing a car park and up to a T-junction with the A3052. Cross the A3052 and

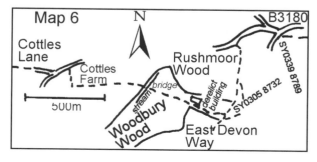

take the road opposite marked 'Woolcombes'. In 30m go through a gate and into Aylesbeare Common RSPB Nature Reserve. Continue along the surfaced road round Harpford Hill and Common ignoring other tracks. Where the road swings left towards Woolcombe Farm buildings after 1km, continue on ahead down a broad track to cross a footbridge over a stream after 300m and in a further 300m to join a surfaced lane, here turn right. In 200m, just after Benchams Cottage turn right onto a footpath. Keeping to the main track on a general bearing of 140 degrees proceed through gorse bushes for 700m. At a cross track go forward for 20m to a stile on the left, SY0754 9001. Cross over the stile and walk across the field, on bearing 10 degrees to a stile in a hedgerow. Cross over the stile and go down the steps, turn right and follow the path with a hedgerow on your right then exit by a hotel entrance.

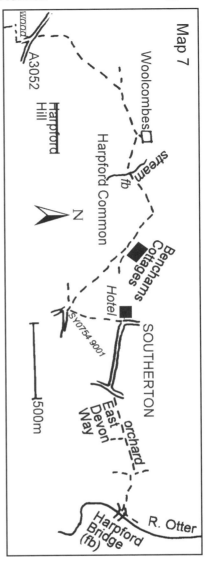

Turn right and walk up to a lane on a bend in 5m. Continue on bearing 100 degrees on the lane ahead. At a T-junction turn left and cross the road and after 10m go through a gate into a field on the right. Continue ahead uphill with the hedgerow on your right. At the top of the hill cross over a stile into an orchard and on ahead through the orchard. In 150m turn left at the far hedgerow and in 40m turn right down steps and on ahead between a hedgerow and another orchard. At the corner of this orchard pass through a kissing gate and down steps into a wooded area. At the bottom of the steps turn right, at the bottom of the next steps turn left and cross over plank bridge then through a kissing gate and into a field. Go on ahead across the field to a stile, plank bridge, kissing gate and another plank bridge and into another field. Cross the field and walk up to Harpford Bridge (*do not cross*) over the River Otter

Harpford Bridge to Ottery St Mary
6.5kms (4.0 miles) Time: 1.75 hrs

L eaving the East Devon Way turn left before the bridge to follow the River Otter. After 450m at the top right-hand corner of the field go through a kissing gate into a field. In 800m at a bridge over the river (*do not cross it*) continue on ahead and follow the river to go through a kissing gate to a road at Tipton St John. Turn left and after 450m, after passing the church of St John the Evangelist and Metcombe Vale, take the footpath on the right through a gate. In 200m turn left through a gate into a field with the River Otter on your right. Pass under a five-arched disused railway bridge and on through a kissing gate.

Follow this riverside path across fields and over plank bridges and stiles for 1.8kms (1.0 miles) to a point where there is a double stile with a plank bridge in between. Cross the plank bridge and take a bearing of 350 degrees away from the river (*a short cut*) regaining the river after 400m. Continue to follow the riverside path through fields and over plank bridges to go under overhead cables and on over plank bridges and stiles. Eventually crossing Millennium Field and then cross over a stile and go up steps to a road.

Here turn right and cross the bridge (St Saviour's Bridge) then cross over the road. Take the footpath on the left immediately after the bridge. Cross over a crossroads with a car park on your left and on ahead passing a Tumbling Weir Mill. Turn right over the footbridge opposite Tumbling Weir Hotel and turn left into a public car park at Ottery St Mary at Land of Canaan. Exit the car park in the right-hand corner to the Land of Canaan, cross the road and walk along Hind Rd. Just before the end of Hind Rd turn left into Saddlers Lane. In 50m turn left into Silver St and walk up to the Church of St Mary in Ottery St Mary.

Gittisham Village

Photo: L Ham

Ottery St Mary to Honiton
12.2kms (7.5 miles) Time: 3.0 hrs

From the Church of St Mary in Ottery St Mary walk to the right of the church along Paternoster Row. At a point where the road turns sharp left, turn right along Ridgeway then pass a cemetery on the left after 600m. After 500m the road becomes a track. In a further 450m go through a gate into a field. Keeping to the right-hand edge of the field go through a gate by a stream and ahead towards Holcombe Barton House. At a junction of tracks amongst farm buildings turn left, and in 400m arrive at a lane.

Here turn right and walk along the lane for 1.3km (0.75 mile), at a single residence take the road to its right then soon up a track amongst trees. Maintain this broad uphill track (which swings right at the top) ignoring paths to left or right. The track descends slowly to a road at SY1330 9663. Here turn left, and in 300m, turn right at a T-junction to walk through Bellevue Plantation area. Follow this single-track lane for 1.8kms (1.0 miles) down to a T-junction in Gittisham village. Here turn right and take the easterly road marked 'Sidmouth'. Keep to this road for 1.4kms (0.75 mile) to a triangle of roads at Beech Walk.

Turn left on a road, bearing 50 degrees, and up to the A375 at SY1540 9890. Turn left and cross over the road (*take care*), in 100m turn right up a single-track road by Roundball Hill. In 900m at a lane (Brand Lane), turn left and just before the end of the lane, turn right up a lane behind residences. Just before the lane joins a road continue on ahead on a footpath to join the road later. Continue on this road (Weatherill Rd) to a junction at a mini-roundabout by St Michael and All Angels' church. Here turn left down Church Hill then into New St and past the railway station and down to a T-junction with High St Honiton.

High Street, Honiton

Photo: L Ham

The route: Westbound

See Special Note on page 49 regarding Topsham to Exeter

Honiton to Ottery St Mary
12.2kms (7.5 miles) Time: 3.0 hrs

From High St/New St in Honiton walk up New St and past the railway station and up Church Hill. At a junction at a mini-roundabout with Weatherill Rd turn right along it. Cross over the road to gain a footpath to a higher level parallel to the road. At a lane continue on in the same direction along it bearing away from Weatherill Rd and down to a T-junction with Brand Lane. Here turn left and in 250m turn right up a lane by Merryfield. After 900m arrive at a T-junction with the A375 by Roundball Hill where turn left. In 100m (*no footpath take care*) bear right down a lane marked 'Gittisham'.

Walk along this lane for 900m up to a junction of lanes at Beech Walk. Turn right down a lane to 'Gittisham' and in 1.4kms (0.75 miles) arrive at a T-junction in Gittisham village. Go forward and just before the bridge over a stream turn left up a lane to pass through Bellevue Plantation area. After 1.8kms (1.0 miles) reach a T-junction where turn left. After 300m where the lane bends left, turn right up a track at Westgate Hill. After 100m take the left fork and later cross over a cross track and on to a T-junction of tracks. Here turn left down the scarp side of the hill overlooking Ottery St Mary.

At the bottom of the track go forward onto a lane. In 1.3kms (0.75 miles) turn left up a track towards Holcombe Barton House. In 400m at a T-junction of tracks in the midst of farm buildings, turn right along a track in a westerly direction. At two gates go through the left-hand one and into a field. Cross the field on the left-hand edge to exit through a gate to a lane, which eventually becomes surfaced. At a junction on a bend go forward in the same direction along Higher Ridgeway. At its end exiting Ridgeway to turn left along Paternoster Rd to follow the road round to the Church of St Mary at Ottery St Mary.

Ottery St Mary from St Mary's Church
Photo: L Ham

Ottery St Mary to Harpford Bridge
6.5kms (4.0 miles) Time: 1.75 hrs

From the Church of St Mary walk away from it down Silver St and before its end turn right along Saddlers Lane and on into Hind Rd. At a T-junction with Land of Canaan, cross over the road and go into a car park. Cross the car park exiting in the left-hand corner over a footbridge opposite the Tumbling Weir Hotel then turn left along a footpath by the River Otter. Cross over a crossroads with a car park on your right and up to a road at a bridge. Cross over the road and turn right over St Saviour's Bridge and turn immediately left down steps to cross Millennium Green with the River Otter now on your left.

Exit Millennium Green over a stile to cross a plank bridge where take the left-hand path to follow the river. Cross over another plank bridge and on ahead. Exit the field over a stile and plank bridge and into another field. In just over 200m where the river turns sharp left continue ahead on bearing about 170 degrees (short cut) to regain the river in 400m to exit the field over a double stile and a plank bridge. Keeping to the riverbank go on ahead over stiles and plank bridges for 1.8kms (1.0 miles) and eventually through a gate and up to a five arched disused brick railway bridge.

Go under an arch and on to exit through a gate in a wooded area. Here turn right and in 200m exit through a gate to a lane. Turn left along Tipton Vale to pass St John the Evangelist church on the right. Before the bridge over the River Otter at Tipton St John, turn right on a footpath. Follow the path ahead across a field to join the riverside path, and in 1.9kms (1.25 miles) ignoring bridges over the river up to Harpford Bridge over the River Otter (*do not cross it*).

Harpford Bridge to Woodbury
11.5kms (7.25 miles) Time: 3.25 hrs

From Harpford Bridge (**Map 7**) (*joining the East Devon Way*) walk away from the bridge across a field on bearing about 290 degrees. Go over a plank bridge, through a kissing gate, and over another plank bridge and into another field. Cross the field in the same direction to go through a kissing gate and over a plank bridge and into a wooded area. Turn right up steps to a higher level then left up steps and through a kissing gate into an orchard. Follow the path ahead with the main orchard on your left to exit in the top right-hand corner up steps and into another orchard.

Here turn left and in 40m turn right to walk through the orchard to the left of a line of windbreak trees. At the top of the orchard go forward over a stile and into a field. Walk down the left-hand side of the field and before the end you may have to cross over a stile (dependent upon field usage at the time) and then in 100m exit through a gate in the bottom left-hand corner to a lane. Turn left and in 10m turn right along a lane marked 'Southerton', quarter of a mile.

After 500m where the lane bends sharp right at a hotel entrance, turn left up a footpath. In 250m the path turns left up steps and into a field. Cross the field uphill on bearing about 200 degrees exiting over a stile to a track. Here turn right and in 25m cross over a cross track and continue on ahead. Keep to this main track ignoring paths to left or right then through gorse bushes in a general direction of 320 degrees and up to the terminal point of a lane by residences. Here turn left passing Benchams Cottages and in 200m turn left up a track.

Cross over a ford on a footbridge and in a further 300m at a T-junction near Woolcombes Farm, on the right, go forward on the surfaced lane.

Maintain this surfaced lane ignoring other tracks to walk round Harpford Common and Harpford Hill. (*From the top of the hill there are good views of Newton Poppleford and the Otter Valley to the left, to the right is Aylesbeare Common*). Arrive at the A3052 at a T-junction where cross over the road and go down the road opposite marked 'Hawkerland'. In 100m turn right down a track and up to a junction of tracks after 200m. Here turn left on a broad track then slowly descending and ignoring other tracks to exit onto a lane where turn right. In 200m at a T-junction turn left and in 100m at a junction of lanes at Hawkerland Cross turn right up a bridleway heading towards the north side of Colaton Raleigh Common crossing it in an overall general direction of about 250 degrees.

In 250m at a junction of tracks take the centre track marked 'East Devon Way' soon passing a low metal iron bar across the track. At a junction area marked 'Fire Point 19' keep to the right-hand broad track leading uphill. Maintain this track slowly ascending to obtain good views of the south coast towards Budleigh Salterton and Exmouth to the left. Passing to the north of a military danger area, arrive at a junction of tracks with a small copse on your right at SY0423 8800. Proceed in the same direction and once within sight of the road ahead bear right along a narrower path. (*The site of Woodbury Castle Fort is to your left*). Soon bear slightly right again and in 200m arrive at a T-junction of roads, on the B3180 (**Map 6**) at SY0339 8789.

Cross over the road and go down the road opposite and in 400m turn left up a bridleway into a wooded area. Maintain this broad track ignoring others and in 500m at a junction of tracks at SY0305 8732 turn right on a downhill track (*leaving the East Devon Way*). Pass a low metal bar barrier and then in 300m a derelict building on the right to proceed on ahead between lines of trees in a forested area. After a dip in the track at a bridge over a stream go ahead through a gate and into a field.

Walk along the right-hand edge of the field to exit through a gate and into another field. In the bottom right-hand corner turn right through the right of two gates and onto a track between hedgerows. Exit to a lane at Cottles Farm where turn left. In 100m at a junction bear right down Cottles Lane and in 700m at a T-junction turn left. After 200m arrive at Parsonage Cross at a T-junction with Pound Lane in Woodbury.

Woodbury to Topsham
7.1kms (4.5 miles) Time: 1.75 hrs

From Parsonage Cross at Pound Lane walk along Pound Lane to a point where it meets Oakhayes Rd on a bend. Turn right on a footpath by Woodbury Centenary allotments. Walk up the right-hand side of the field exiting in the top right-hand corner to another field. Maintain direction to exit the field in the top right-hand corner over a stile to a lane. Here turn left and in 5m up to Bond's Lane where turn right, by 'Buckfield'. After 200m turn left through a large gap in the hedgerow and into a field. Walk along the right-hand edge of the field by the hedgerow. Follow the hedgerow round a sharp right angle and in 200m exit over a stile to a lane on a bend near Pilehayes Farm.

Here turn immediately left along an unsurfaced track (Moor Lane). After 1.2kms (0.75 miles) arrive at a lane, where turn left along it, and then on to a T-junction with the B3179 in 400m. Here turn right and in 30m turn left down a lane marked 'Ebford' three quarters of a mile. After 150m at a T-junction turn right and in a further 800m at a T-junction turn left along Lower Lane. In 500m up to a T-junction in Ebford village where turn right along Old Ebford Lane. After 250m at a junction with the A376 cross over the road and go down the lane opposite.

At the end of the lane turn right to walk between residences and onto a footpath to the right of a house gate to walk alongside a stream and up to a road. Turn left and walk along the roadside footpath for 800m crossing over the River Clyst and up the hill. At the top of the hill just after Elm Grove School turn left along a path to cross over an active railway line (*take care*) near Topsham railway station then exit to a road. Turn left to soon walk along Parsons Path alongside the road passing a footbridge over the road and on along Holman Way then go forward to the quayside at Topsham.

Topsham to Exeter
8.0kms (5.0 miles) Time: 2.0 hrs

Special Note: Although walking part of this leg is possible at low tide, it remains wet and slippery and might be a problem to those walkers carrying heavy backpacks. On this leg it is NOT advisable to walk it at high tide or when the River Exe is in flood. An alternative route round a 1.4km section is advised, see below.

From the quayside at Topsham walk in a northerly direction alongside the River Exe along Strand passing the Topsham Ferry. Follow this road into Ferry Rd to where it joins Ashford Rd. (**At this point take the detour route (below) if it is wet, high tide or the River Exe is in flood.**) Continue across Topsham Playing Fields and follow the path which becomes a ledge above the river and passes by the Retreat Boatyard and then under the M5 motorway before cutting across a raised reed bed on the riverbank to regain the landside after 1.2kms (0.75 miles). At a clearing turn right and in 40m turn left **(Detour route re-joins here)** and go up steps to walk behind residences.

*Detour route: On Ferry Rd and before Topsham Playing Fields turn right along Ashford Rd and up to a T-junction. Turn left along Exeter Rd and pass under the M5 motorway and on into Topsham Rd. In a further 400m turn left on a footpath to walk behind residences. Exit to an open space where turn left through a gate to rejoin the main path from the river. Turn right up steps to rejoin the path. **End of detour.** (Go back to end of last paragraph).*

Exit the path over a stile by residences and down to a road. Here turn left and walk along Glasshouse Lane and up to the A379. Cross over the road and on ahead on Countess Wear Rd passing Mount Wear House youth hostel and Countess Wear House built in 1715 with Bell Tower and Weather Vane. In a dip in the road turn left along Mill Rd, an unsurfaced lane which soon becomes surfaced. In 200m turn left down Mill Lane and into Riverside Valley Park soon passing the ruins of Countess Wear Paper Mills (1638-1885).

When the lane swings left turn right through a gate on a footpath alongside a stream which then bears right round a golf course. At a footbridge turn left across it and up to a road. Cross the road and go forward up a track ahead. At a Y-junction take the right-hand path between St Loyes College and up to a lane at a bend, here turn left. Then go onto a narrower lane to regain the riverside and on to exit the Riverside Valley Park nearby a footbridge on the left.

Here turn right up a lane and walk round behind residences and to a road. Cross the road between Old Abbey Court and Salmonpool Lane and on ahead on an enclosed footpath to regain the riverside path. Follow this path alongside the River Exe passing the old Trews Weir Mill on the right, now converted to flats, and Trews Weir on the left. Beyond Port Royal Inn go through a metal gate and soon to the Exeter Quayside, passing the old fish market and Custom House on the right. Continue along to just before the first of the twin road bridges, here gain street level, through pedestrian subway with directions to Fore St and turn right to gain access across the old medieval bridge and the West Gate ruins. (*Prince William would have entered the city this way*).

Exiting the West Gate ruins continue on ahead into West St on the left passing the Old House (*that was moved, note nearby plaque on wall to William's entry into Exeter*) on the left. Cross over West St and go up Stepcote Hill (beside St Mary Steps Church with Matthew Miller clock) then ahead into Smythen St. At a T-junction with Market St turn left and soon reach Fore St. Here turn right and at a crossroads of Fore St, High St, North St and South St go half-right through a covered entranceway and into the area of Exeter Cathedral and on up to the Cathedral.

Honiton to Beaminster

Map: OS Explorer 115 and 116
Start: High St/New St Honiton
Finish: The Square Beaminster
Distance: 44.5kms (28.0 miles)
Time: 13.0 hrs
Transport: Railway: Honiton, Axminster
Buses: Honiton, Dalwood (infrequently), Axminster, Hawkchurch (infrequently), Stoke Abbott, Beaminster
Place of historical interest: Parnham House Beaminster

Special Note: On this section after Hawkchurch refreshments are only available at Stoke Abbot 17.2kms (11.0 miles) from Hawkchurch and 4kms (2.5 miles) from Beaminster.

Special Note: On the Honiton to Axminster leg the crossing of the ford at Umborne Brook may be a problem in the event of very wet weather. An alternative route avoiding the ford is given. In the Eastbound direction it is important to make the decision to take the alternative route at Four Cross. The total distance of the alternative route is about 2.5kms (1.5 miles).

The history

Prince William marched to Axminster from Honiton on the 22ⁿᵈ November. It was a short march but a difficult one due to the weather. Heavy rain, driven by a strong cold wind had caused the low ground between the Rivers Axe and Yarty to become flooded and the troops were up to their knees and sometimes their thighs in water. The Army, who had to billet around the town where they could, overwhelmed Axminster. Axminster was too small to accommodate William's swelling forces, which had to be billeted far and wide around the town in surrounding villages. It is thought that William lodged in the Dolphin Inn whilst in Axminster.

As mentioned in Chapman's – *A History of Axminster*:

'Pulman states that William 'put up' at the Dolphin Inn, which seems highly likely as it was then the town's premier inn and a posting station. It was a big, rambling building, three storeys high, with many rooms, annexes and stables that would have served admirably as a military headquarters. Futhermore it stood in the centre of the town, on the east side of the old market place at the top of Castle Hill, in direct touch with William's lines of communication'.

It was in Axminster that Prince William revealed his penchant for real ale when he complained that his Breda ale had not arrived from Holland, when it did he complained it tasted salty.

Whilst in Axminster William received the boost to his cause by the desertion of Lord John Churchill, King James's most able commander, together with some of his troops. This was a severe blow to the King and most likely spelled the end as others followed in their defection to William.

John Churchill, 1st Duke of Marlborough
Possibly by John Closterman, 1660-1691
© *National Portrait Gallery*

On the same day a 'Declaration of the Nobility, Gentry, and Commonalty at the Rendezvous at Nottingham' was issued, which meant even more support for Prince William. York also declared for the Prince on the 22 November.

On the 23 November Prince William's brother in law Prince George of Denmark, who was married to Anne, wrote a letter to his father in law, James II, explaining his actions for deserting him and attaching himself to the Prince of Orange. This was of no great loss to James and no great gain to Prince William as Prince George was thought of as an amiable dimwit. Prince George, of

James II
By Sir Godfrey Kneller, 1646-1723
© *National Portrait Gallery*

whom Charles II had said of him 'I have tried Prince George sober, and I have tried him drunk, and drunk or sober, there is nothing in him.' The effect on James when he further heard of Anne being spirited away from Whitehall on the 25 November became too much for him, who, it is said, burst into tears, saying, 'God help me! My own children have forsaken me.'

The march through Beaminster was marred by the poisoning of a few of William's troops at a Catholic household, it is generally thought to have taken place at Parnham House, when the owner invited some of William's straggling troops to a meal of meat and ale, which he had poisoned. A short distance after leaving the house they became ill, later one soldier died during the night. Rev Whittle tells us:

Mary of Modena, James II's queen
By William Wissing, 1656-1687
© National Portrait Gallery

'Near to Beminster there lived a Gentleman, whos Name I shall forbear, but a very rigid Papist, and one whom I cannot quite forget, because of his unkindness and curs'd Intention towards the Army: Hearing that some Regiments would pass that way, he resolved to give some their last Meat And Drink (as his own neighbours at Beminster informed us when we were there) therefore he caused a Beef or two to be kill'd and poison'd the Flesh, making it into Pyes; and poison'd also a Hogshead or two of Beer, and as much of Sider, for the hungry Souldiers (as he call'd them) against they came that way. Some of his Neighbours hearing of this cursed Design, spread it purposely about the Country, to prevent any of the Prince of Orange's Men from being destroyed; insomuch that every Regiment was timely warn'd hereof: But as in all great Armies, there will be some Straglers, so there were some in ours, tho' not many; and these not hearing of this Bait, accidentally passed that way; and as they approached near the House, they concluded 'twas their best course to call and drink [there] because it shew'd well to the Eye, and the People all along were very kind to the Souldiers, , and would make them drink, and in many Places eat; Hereupon these Straglers went to the house and asked for some Beer; and the people there made them eat and drink freely, saying Their Master had provided for them. After they had eat and drank, they hastned towards their Regiments, lest the Enemies Party should happen to meet them; Being come a little more than a quarter of a mile from the house, they grew so suddenly so weak and faint, that they were not able to go any farther; so they laid down under a Tree, not suspecting what was the matter. As they were in this desperate condition, by meer Providence there came a Surgeon-Major that way, who espying some Souldiers (supposed they were some of Prince of Orange's Men) he went to speak with them; and seeing them look so fearfully (their Eyes being prodigiously swell'd) he ask'd presently, What was the matter with them? Or what did ail them? They told him, they knew not, only that they had eat and drink at the Gentleman's House behind (pointing to the House); The Surgeon, having heard of their evil Preparations, prepared immediately an Antidote, and gave directions what they must do; Whereupon they presently began to vomit, and after some time they waxed a little better, and made shift to get to the Waggons which carried sick Souldiers, and were under the Surgeon-Majors hands for some time. At the very next Town, called Yetminster, one Souldier died in the Night, and no one could tell what was the matter with him, being very well when he went to bed, which Souldier I buried there according to our Liturgy. The others that were poisoned, were strangely altered, their Eyes being swell'd in an odd manner'

The route: Eastbound

Honiton to Axminster
17.0kms (10.5 miles) time: 5.0 hrs

From the T-junction of High St/New St walk east along the High St (A35). At a roundabout turn right into Kings Rd. After crossing a railway bridge turn left into Hale Lane. After 250m go through a gate and on into a field and on ahead with a hedgerow on your left. At the top left-hand corner walk between hedgerows on a track. After 200m go through a gate turn right and then left through Hale Farm buildings then through another gate and on ahead.

After 90m where the track bears right go left at about 80 degrees following the hedgerow to the edge of a wood on your left. Keep to the edge of the wood on bearing of about 50 degrees and walk to the left-hand corner of the field, cross over two stiles by a gate and into a field and continue on in the same direction. Go through a line of trees and into another field and underneath power cables. In the bottom left-hand corner of the field, cross over a stile to a track at ST1839 0105 and turn right. After 250m at Hutgate Rd turn left.

Walk along the grass verge of the road and after 600m at a T-junction marked 'Cotleigh' turn right. In 1km and just after Cleverhayes Farm turn right on a footpath at ST1976 0170 (**Map 8**) between hedgerows. Emerging after 600m at a cross lane (Four Cross) (*To avoid crossing the ford at Umborne Brook. Turn left along the lane towards Cotleigh. After 750m turn right at a T-junction. Go through village passing the church and in a further 600m cross the Umborne Brook at a bridge. Turn immediately right on waymarked path alongside the brook. Follow the path for about 1km to emerge at the ford down some steps. To re-join the path continue on ahead*), proceed forward on the lane opposite. Passing Southcote Farm go forward down a stony track between hedgerows eventually to the ford at Umbourne Brook after 500m at ST2123 0121.

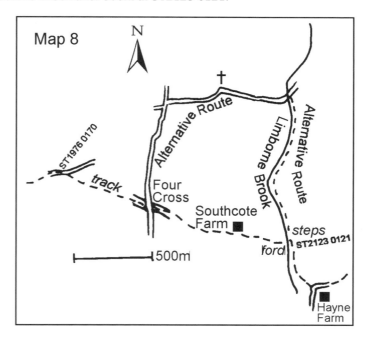

Cross the Umbourne Brook and follow the path to the right and uphill away from the brook exiting to a lane at Hayne Farm. Here turn left up the sometimes steep lane to a T-junction opposite Stockland Hill TV Station. Here turn right and after 800m at Lamb Farm (**Map 9**), take the footpath on the left, cross a plank over a ditch and into field following the right-hand hedgerow. In the bottom right-hand corner cross over a stile and on ahead. At the bottom right hand corner cross a stile and into a field. Exit through a gate to go over a crosstrack, then go up steps and over a stile and into a field. Cross the field in the same direction to a point underneath the power cables at ST2281 0079, then turn right.

Proceed alongside the hedgerow and go through a gate at the left-hand corner of the field and on ahead with the hedgerow on your left. Go through a gate and on ahead. At the bottom left-hand corner go through a gate into another field. After 30m joining a path from the left by a gate, continue ahead. In the left-hand corner of the field go through a gate into another field continuing ahead. At the bottom left-hand corner of the field go through a small gate into another field. Continue downhill with a hedgerow on your left to go through a gap in a hedgerow and into another field. In the bottom left-hand corner cross over a stile into another field. Turn immediately left then right to follow a hedgerow on the right and down to pass by dwellings, then emerging at a lane (Ham Rd).

Cross over the lane and go through a gate into a field. Walk down the left-hand side of the field exiting through a gap in the hedgerow and into another field. Continue on in same direction, then crossing over a footbridge and into another field. Passing the village church on the right, exit the field through a gate and into a small car park. Cross the car park half right and turn left on a path behind a building. In 30m turn right up to a lane in Dalwood village.

Turn left over a bridge over Corry Brook. In 50m where the road turns left continue ahead

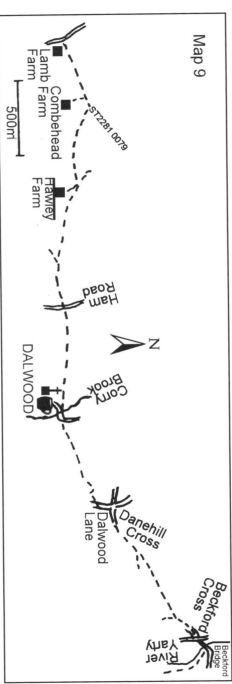

up a concrete public footpath. After a few metres, at farm buildings, turn left through a gate and immediately turn right keeping to the right-hand edge of the field and on through a gate into another field. Go uphill across the field and then cross over a stile in a small neck of the field. Turn left following the hedgerow. In the top left-hand corner of the field go through a gate and into a field, continue on to cross a plank over a ditch and a stile in a hedgerow. Turn right, then immediately left uphill to a concrete lane by residences, here turn right and follow it uphill to a lane where turn left. After 100m at a junction of four roads (Danehill Cross) turn right up Dalwood Lane.

After passing cottages in 300m take a path through a gate on the left. Head across the field away from the hedgerow at about 60 degrees exiting over a stile in a hedgerow and into another field. Continue downhill on the right-hand edge of the field exiting by a double gate by a dwelling, turn left and walk up to a crossroads at Beckford Cross. Cross over road and walk along the lane opposite then cross over the concrete bridge over the River Yarty. (*The former stone arch Beckford Bridge is to the left.*)

Immediately after crossing the bridge take the public footpath on the right and follow the bank of the River Yarty now heading at about 160 degrees towards Axminster. Cross over a gated plank-bridge and continue ahead exiting the field through a gap in the hedgerow and into another field. Exit through a gate in a hedgerow and into another field. Cross into a smaller field and on through a gap in the hedgerow and into another field continuing on ahead. Cross a bridge over a stream and on over a stile in a tree line and into another small field and on ahead to Higher Westwater farm buildings.

Keeping to the right of the farm buildings arrive at a footbridge over the River Yarty (*Do not cross*). Proceed on ahead over a stile into a field and on ahead. Cross over a stile and plank-bridge in a line of trees, then a second stile and into a field. Bear left to a stile by a hedgerow and up to a dwelling where turn left to join a lane. Turn right along the lane for 100m to a T-junction to 'Middle West Water' (*Here you may continue along the lane as the path re-joins the lane further along at the T-junction to Westwater Farm*). Go up the steps on the right and over a stile and over a second stile in 20m. Exit onto a driveway of a residence. Turn right up the driveway to pass through the front of the residence and on through a gate to a small field.

Exit over a stile to a small field then go through a gate and into another field. Walk alongside the left-hand hedgerow parallel to the lane exiting over a stile in the left-hand corner to the lane at a T-junction signed to 'Westwater Farm'. Continue ahead along the lane in same direction and up to an offset crossroads (Fourway Cross). Turn right then immediately left and on towards Axminster down Fourcross Hill. After 900m cross over a stone bridge over the River Axe and then a railway level crossing and on up Castle Hill. Before the top turn right into Castle St and up to West St and across the road to The Minster Church of St Mary the Virgin, in Trinity Square, Axminster.

Axminster to Hawkchurch
6.3kms (4.0 miles) Time: 2.0 hrs

From The Minster Church of St Mary the Virgin, in Trinity Square, Axminster take the Chard road A358 out of town to a point where it joins the B326 at a T-junction. Cross over the road and take a public footpath opposite towards Millbrook. After 100m cross over a stile and into a field. In the top left-hand corner cross over a stile and into another field following the hedgerow to another stile in a hedgerow, continue on ahead to a gap in a hedge. Go up the field then veer left towards the farm buildings to exit over a stile in a hedgerow (*there are two stiles in this hedgerow 30m apart make sure you go over the left one*). Turn left and go through the farmyard exiting through a gate and onto a track heading due north. At a T-junction at a lane turn right. After 200m where the lane swings left continue ahead on public bridleway (Evil Lane).

Walk along Evil Lane for 1km to exit to Cuthays Lane, here turn left. After 330m go through a gate on the right to Cuthays Farm. Go right and left between farm buildings exiting through a gate into a field. In the left-hand corner of the field go through the right-hand gate of two and continue along the right-hand edge of field exiting to a lane (Lodge Lane), here turn right passing Pendragon Cottage. After 60m take the left-hand track going downhill. After 600m where a farm track (Old Barn Farm) comes in from the right go through a gate on the left on bearing about 60 degrees down across a field.

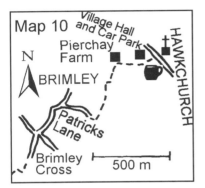

After 300m go through a gate and cross a plank bridge over a stream and then heading uphill to the left of a line of trees to exit through a gate and in a few metres round to a lane (Langmoor Lane), here turn left. At a crossroads (Brimley Cross) (**Map 10**) go forward towards Brimley. At a T-junction in 250m turn right uphill and in 200m turn left through a gate and into a field crossing it at about 30 degrees exiting at the top left-hand corner through a gate and across another field and up to Piercehay Farm. Go through a gate and through the farmyard exiting through a gate into a field to the left of a barn.

Go ahead through a gap in a hedgerow and into another field and in 50m to a stile on the right. Cross over the stile and into a field. Keeping to the left of the field exit at the top left-hand corner over a stile and into a small field to go past dwellings and on past the village hall and car park and up to a lane. Turn right and walk up to St John the Baptist church in Hawkchurch.

Hawkchurch to Sadborow Pound
5.5kms (3.5 miles) Time: 1.5hrs

From St John the Baptist church in Hawkchurch walk along a path to the left of the church exiting through the left of two gates and on ahead. In 200m at a junction of cross paths go through the gate ahead and continue straight on ahead on the grassy track (bridleway) turning left through a gate at ST3478 0050 signed 'Monarch's Way'. Go down the field alongside a hedgerow and a residence on the right. Where the hedgerow goes right around the residence go forward across the field to exit over a stile by a gate. Cross the field and exit over a stile by a gate and into another field. Here turn right to follow the right-hand edge of the field down to a footbridge over a stream and across another field and up to a lane on a bend at ST3538 0122.

Turn left up the lane towards Beerhall Farm and in 150m turn right through a gate and into a field. Turn left up the field and veer right to join a track from the farm at the top of the field. Turn right on bearing generally 90 degrees across the tops of several fields exiting to a lane at ST3604 0135 just south of Yonder Farm. Here turn left and in 600m turn right down a bridleway between residences passing Willow Lodge on the right.

At Elmore Farm walk through the farmyard and on ahead into a field crossing it at about 70 degrees exiting to another field. Maintain bearing of about 90 degrees across fields towards Home Farm passing to the right and south of Sadborow. Join a track and maintaining the same direction walk up to a lane on a bend at ST3749 0188. Here

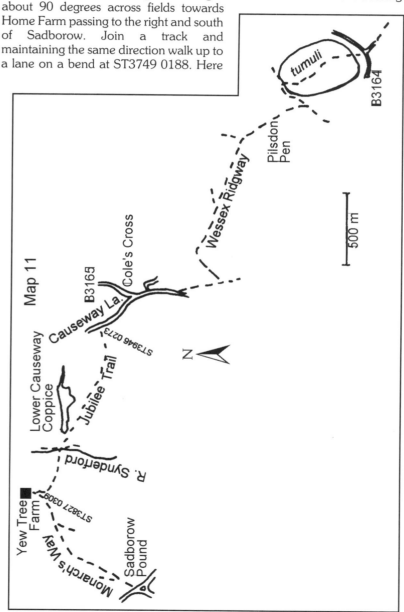

turn left and in 600m up to Sadborow Pound T-junction. (*To avoid lane walking for most of that 600m you can, after a few metres along the lane, turn left into the main driveway of Sadborow, then in 30m turn right to walk alongside the edge of the field for 450m exiting through a gate to re join the lane*).

Sadborow Pound to Pilsdon Pen
6.2kms (4.0 miles) Time: 2.0 hrs

From Sadborow Pound T-junction (**Map 11**) turn left and cross the road and go through a gate and onto a track on bearing about 25 degrees. In 500m go through a gate and into a field to follow the track round to the right. Exit through a gate to go downhill to exit through a gate to Yew Tree Farm at ST3827 0309.

Here turn sharp right into a field and continue to its bottom edge to go over a stile and into a wooded area. Go down through the wood to cross a footbridge over a stream (River Synderford) exiting into a field to continue up the left-hand edge. Exit over a stile and into a field crossing at about 120 degrees. Exit through a gate into another field then over a double stile into another field to cross at about 130 degrees. Exit through a gate into a field keeping to the left-hand edge to exit through a gate into another field and over a stile in a hedgerow and up to a lane (Causeway Lane) at ST3946 0273.

Here turn right along the lane for 300m to a T-junction with the B3165 at Cole's Cross. Here turn right and in 375m turn left on a track soon to go through a gate and on ahead on the right-hand side of the field. Exit in the right-hand corner through the left of two gates and onto a track. In 10m turn left through a gate and onto a track round the left edge of a field first on bearing about 50 degrees then soon about 110 degrees along with the Wessex Ridgeway. Exit over a stile by a gate and on ahead aiming for the left of two

View from the tumuli at Pilsdon Pen

Photo: L Ham

gates to cross over a stile and onto a permissive footpath. Then ahead keeping to the right-hand side of the field to exit over a double stile and into another field.

Cross the field on a bearing of about 140 degrees to the right hand edge exiting before the end of the field over a stile by a gate and into another field. Continue down the field to the bottom left-hand corner to exit in an area of three gates to turn immediately left and back up a track to Pilsdon Pen. In 150m at the summit turn right to cross the Tumuli and pass the Trig Point and on down the steep main track to exit over a stile to a road (B3164).

Pilsdon Pen to Beaminster
9.5kms (6.0 miles) Time: 2.5 hrs

From the stile at Pilsdon Pen and the B3164 turn left along the road for 50m to a T-junction where turn right. Walk down the lane for 700m to go past a T-junction and in a further 600m where the lane turns right at ST4228 9997. Turn left onto a track and in 250m go through a gate and into a field and on ahead through a gap in a hedgerow to another field. Cross the field on bearing 80 degrees to exit over a stile and a farm access track (Laverstock Farm), then continue on ahead across another field maintaining the same direction. Exit through a gate and immediately go over a stile on the right and into a field crossing at about 80 degrees.

Exit through a gap in the hedgerow and into another field crossing at about 120 degrees exiting over a stile and into a wooded area. Cross over a plank footbridge then bear right up some steps to cross over a stile exiting the wooded area and into a field. Here turn left and in 100m when the hedgerow swings left continue on ahead uphill to the top of the field to exit through a gate and into another field. Cross the field on bearing about 90 degrees to the top right hand corner to exit through a gate and onto a lane. Here turn left along the lane and in 300m up to a road junction with the B3162 at Four Ashes.

Cross over the B3162 and continue on the lane

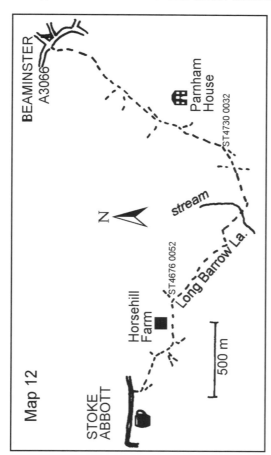

opposite to Stoke Abbott. In 500m at a left-hand bend by Brimley Cottages turn right on a track and round to the left passing the cottages. Go on ahead onto a track between hedgerows. Go through a kissing gate and into a field. Go down the field on bearing about 110 degrees to exit into a wooded area crossing over a footbridge and over a stile into a field. Here turn half-left uphill to exit over a stile and access track to a residence to go forward up steps and over a stile and into a field. Go forward to cross a stile into another field and on ahead to exit through a gate to a lane.

Here turn left and in 60m up to a lane at a bend, continue on in the same direction along the lane and through Stoke Abbott village (**Map 12**). 150m past the New Inn at 'Flaxhayes' turn right through a gate along a concrete footpath between residences exiting over a stile and into an irregular shaped field. Go down the field bearing round to the left to cross over a footbridge and into another field. Here turn left exiting over a footbridge and into a wooded area. Eventually passing residences on the left, and down to a track. Here turn left for 5m and then right through a gate to cross the corner of a field.

In 40m cross over a stile in a line of trees then over a footbridge to exit into a scrubby field. Cross the field exiting over a stile in a hedgerow and into another field. Here go half-left exiting in the top right hand corner through a gap to another field. Walk along the left-hand edge of the field for 40m exiting over a stile on the left to Long Barrow Lane at ST4626 0052.

Here turn right along Long Barrow Lane, after 500m the track swings left before a gate and on for another 100m exiting through a gate and into a field. Cross the field on bearing about 120 degrees exiting in the bottom right-hand corner into a wooded area to cross over a footbridge. Go through this wooded area alongside a stream to pass a footbridge on the right (*do not cross*), continue round to the left and go through a gate into a field. Cross the field on bearing about 70 degrees to exit over a stile in a hedgerow at a lane.

Cross the lane diagonally left and in 5m go through a kissing gate at ST4730 0032 into a field, then slowly descend to the right hand edge of the field. At a double line of trees across the path turn right through a kissing gate to a track by the grounds of Parnham House. Here turn left along the track ignoring other tracks to cross over a stile by a gate. Proceeding on ahead to and exit through a gate into another field and on ahead on the right-hand side of the field. Exit through a gate and onto a track which becomes a lane and onto St Mary Well St. At a T-junction turn right up Church St and up to The Square at Beaminster.

The route: Westbound

Special Note: On this section after Stoke Abbot refreshments are only available at Hawkchurch 17.2kms (11.0 miles) from Beaminster and 4.0kms (2.5 miles) from Axminster.

Beaminster to Pilsdon Pen
9.5kms (6.0 miles) Time: 2.5 hrs

From The Square at Beaminster (**Map 12**) walk west down Church St. Turn left along St Mary Well St. In 150m at a Y-junction of paths continue on the right-hand lane ahead which soon becomes a track. At the end of the track where it becomes a private road go through a gate to proceed in the same direction. Exit through a gate and into another field to slowly cross over to the right-hand side. Exit over a stile by a gate to take the right hand track uphill by the grounds of Parnham House.

After 300m turn right through a kissing gate at ST4730 0032 and into a field where immediately turn left. Cross the field exiting through a kissing gate in the middle of a hedgerow to cross a farm track to go left over a stile diagonally opposite and into a field. Cross the field on bearing about 260 degrees heading for a line of trees across a dip at the bottom end of the field. Go through a gate and into a wooded area. In 40m pass a footbridge on the left (do not cross) and continue on alongside a stream to cross over a footbridge and into a field.

Cross the field on bearing of about 320 degrees to exit through a gate in the top left-hand corner and onto a track (Long Barrow Lane). In 100m follow the lane sharp right and in a further 500m at ST4626 0052 turn left over a stile in the hedgerow and into a field. Here turn right and in 40m go through a gap into another field crossing it diagonally half-left to exit over a stile to a scrubby field. Cross the field exiting through bushes into a wooded area. Go down to cross a footbridge and through a gate to a field. Cross the corner of the field exiting through a gate in 40m at a track.

Immediately through the gate turn left on a track for 5m then turn right into the wooded area soon to bear left uphill passing residences on the right. Exit the wood over a footbridge and into a field. Cross the field keeping to the right-hand edge exiting before the corner over a footbridge on the right into a small irregular shaped hilly field. Here turn left, then bear right up the field to exit through a kissing gate by residences and through a gate at a lane, Flaxhayes. Here turn left and continue through Stoke Abbott village for 700m.

Where the lane turns sharp right, go up the track ahead, and in 60m turn right through a gate and into a field. Cross the field exiting over a stile and into another field and on ahead. Exit over a stile in a line of trees then go down some steps to cross an access road to a residence. Cross over a stile and into a field and on down half-right to exit over a stile into a wooded area. Cross over a footbridge and into a field where go half-left up the field on bearing about 290 degrees. Exit through a kissing gate in the top left hand corner by Brimley Farm buildings and onto a track between hedgerows and up to a lane at a bend by Brimley Cottages.

Here turn left along the lane for 500m to a road junction with the B3162 at Four Ashes. Cross over the B3162 and continue up the lane opposite for a further 300m to ST4370 0019. Here turn right through a gate and into a field crossing on bearing about 270 degrees. Exit in the bottom right hand corner through a gate and into another field. Continue down the field aiming to join the right hand hedgerow at a corner. Follow the hedgerow for a further 100m and at ST4312 0018 turn right over a stile and down steps into a wooded area.

Then bearing round to the left to cross over a plank bridge and up to a stile and into a field. Cross the field on bearing about 290 degrees exiting in 130m through a gap in the hedgerow and into another field, to cross half-left on bearing about 260 degrees. Exit over a stile and immediately go left through a gate to cross a field in the same direction (260 degrees).

At a farm access track (Laverstock Farm) cross over and go over a stile into a field crossing at about 250 degrees to exit through a gap in a tree line and into a small field. Cross the field and in 40m go through a gate and onto a track between trees. In 250m go up to a lane on a bend. Here turn right along the lane for 1.3kms (0.75 mile) and up to a road, the B3164. Here turn left and in 50m up to a stile on the right at the foot of Pilsdon Pen.

Pilsdon Pen to Sadborow Pound
6.2kms (4.0 miles) Time: 2.0 hrs

From the stile at the foot of Pilsdon Pen on the B3164 (**Map 11**) go over the stile and follow the steep main track to the top of the hill. Passing the Trig Point walk across the top of the Tumuli in a northerly direction for 400m exiting through the ramparts to a cross track. Here turn left to go round the edge of the hill fort soon to go downhill to a point at ST4104 0133 by a gate.

Turn right through the gate then left and right again within a few metres to enter a field. Cross the field back uphill on bearing about 350 degrees exiting over a stile and into another field. Heading across the field on bearing about 330 degrees for 400m to exit over a double stile into another field. Cross the field on the left-hand side along a line of trees exiting over a stile and into another field. Cross the field exiting over a stile and into another field to continue ahead on the right hand edge on a track.

Follow the track round to the left and down to exit through a gate. Here turn right and in 10m go through a gate into a field. Walk along the left-hand edge of the field exiting after 250m through a gate on the left and up to a lane, the B3165 at ST3970 0216. Here turn right along the lane and after 400m, turn left at a Y-junction (Cole's Cross) up Causeway Lane. In 300m at ST3946 0272 turn left over a stile and enter a field.

Go down the field exiting in the right hand corner through a gate and into another field. Keeping to the right hand side exiting in the right hand corner through a gate into another field. Cross the corner of the field at about 310 degrees exiting over a double stile in the hedgerow. Proceed in the same direction exiting in the left-hand corner through a gate to another field. Cross the field on bearing about 300 degrees to exit over a stile in the right-hand corner and into another field.

Go down the right hand edge of the field, exiting in the corner over a footbridge and on ahead through a wooded area and in 80m up to a stile and into a field. Aiming to the left of Yew Tree Farm buildings to exit at the top of the field through a gate and to a track at ST3827 0309. Here turn sharp left on a track initially on bearing about 220 degrees. Continue on ignoring other tracks to go through a gate into a field. Follow the track round to the left and through a gate and on ahead for 500m exiting through a gate at a T-junction of lanes at Sadborow Pound.

Sadborow Pound to Hawkchurch
5.5kms (3.5 miles) Time: 1.5 hrs

From Sadborow Pound walk south along the lane to Sadborow for 600m. (*To avoid this lane walk, after 150m turn right through a gate into a field and walk down the left-hand edge parallel to the lane. Where it meets the driveway to Sadborow, turn left and exit the grounds to rejoin the lane, then turn right for a few metres*). At Home Farm turn right along a path at ST3749 0188 on bearing about 270 degrees to cross fields south of Sadborow. After crossing three fields go through Elsmore Farm exiting to a bridleway and up to a lane by residences (Willow Lodge on left). Here turn left and in 600m turn right through a gate at ST3604 0135 and into a field.

Cross several fields along the top edge bearing left just before Beerhall Farm to exit through a gate to a lane. Here turn left and in 150m at a bend turn right through a gate at ST3538 0122 to cross a field exiting over a footbridge and up into another field. Before the end of the field turn left over a stile by a gate. Go forward across the field to join a hedgerow by a residence on the left and up to a gate at ST3478 0050. Here turn right on a grassy track (bridleway) exiting through a gate at ST3452 0057 to a track. Follow the track ahead to go through a gate and enter the churchyard of St John the Baptist. Exit the churchyard to a lane in Hawkchurch.

Hawkchurch to Axminster
6.3kms (4.0 miles) Time: 2.0 hrs

Exiting from St John the Baptist churchyard in Hawkchurch (**Map 10**) turn right along the lane and in 50m turn left on a footpath passing the village hall and car park and go into a field. Cross the field and then go over a stile in the right-hand corner and into another field. Turn right and go down the right hand edge of the field to go over another stile in the corner and into another field. Here turn left and go through a gate into the farmyard of Piercehay Farm.

Cross the farmyard and exit through a gate opposite and into a field. Walk down the left-hand side of the field and then through a gate and into another field. Bear right down the field to the bottom left-hand corner to exit through a gate to a lane (Patricks Lane), here turn right. At a T-junction near residences turn left along a lane. At Brimley Cross crossroads go forward down the lane opposite (Langmoor Lane). In 300m at a cross track of footpaths turn right along a track and in 80m go through a gate into a field. Go down the field initially by a bank with a tree line. At the end of the tree line go forward down the field soon bearing slightly right towards the bottom of the field.

Cross over a footbridge over a stream and go on up into a field. Cross the field on bearing about 240 degrees exiting to a track on a bend. Here turn right and follow this track for 600m steadily uphill to a T-junction of tracks. Turn right onto a surfaced lane by Pendragon Cottage. Opposite the cottage turn left through a gate along a footpath across the left-hand side of a field. Exit through a gate to proceed on the right-hand side of the next field aiming for Cuthay's Farm buildings. Cross another very small field then through a gate and go round a farmhouse to exit through a gate and then go round to the left and onto an unsurfaced track.

Follow this track for 300m to exit through a gate and onto a surfaced lane ahead. After 350m turn right down a bridleway soon passing a large cowshed and then on ahead along a track called Evil Lane. The track narrows later and then broadens again and after 1.1kms (0.75 miles) exits through a gate to a surfaced lane at a bend. Continue on in the same direction and in 200m turn left up a broad footpath to enter a farmyard through a gate.

Go slightly right through the farmyard down the side of farm buildings and in 20m turn right over a stile and into a field. Cross the field bearing slightly left exiting through a gap in a hedgerow and across another field. Go over a stile and planks and into another field and head off slightly left to join a hedgerow at a corner point, then walk alongside it in the same direction to exit the field over a stile by cottages. Go forward and up to a road, the A358, here turn left and at Stoney Lane cross over it and turn left up Chard Rd and into Chard St continuing on into Axminster centre and up to The Minster Church of St Mary the Virgin, in Trinity Square, Axminster.

Axminster to Honiton
17.0kms (10.5 miles) time: 5.0 hrs

From The Minster Church of St Mary the Virgin in Trinity Square, Axminster. Cross over West St to a point where Castle St leads off to the left. Go down Castle St to a T-junction with Castle Hill, here turn left. At the bottom of Castle Hill go forward over the railway level crossing and then over a bridge over the River Axe. Continue on the lane ahead and in 1km up to Fourway Cross, on offset junction of four lanes. Turn right and then left on a lane marked 'Westwater'.

In 500m and just after a T-junction to Westwater Farm (*here you may continue along the lane as the path re-joins the lane further along at the T-junction to Westwater Farm*) go over a stile on the left and into a field. Turn right and walk alongside the hedgerow parallel to the lane. Exit the field in the bottom right-hand corner through a gate and into another small field. Exit over a stile by a residence. Go through a gate and cross through the residence and down their access drive. Before the end of the drive turn left over a stile and in 20m go over another stile and down steps to regain the lane at a T-junction marked to 'Middle West Water'.

Continue along the lane for 100m to go through a gate on the left by a residence to maintain direction parallel with the lane. In 60m go over a stile and into a field. Cross the field bearing left at about 310 degrees to cross a stile and then a footbridge to gain the course of the River Yarty on the left. Follow the course of the river ahead across a field exiting over a stile by a footbridge over the river at 'Higher Westwater' (*Do not cross the footbridge*).

Continue on ahead crossing fields alongside the River Yarty over stiles, through gates and over footbridges for 2kms (1.25 miles) to arrive at a lane at Beckford Bridge (**Map 9**). Here turn left along the lane crossing the bridge over the River Yarty. (*The former stone Beckford Bridge is 30m on the right*).

In 150m at Beckford Cross, go forward on the unmetalled road opposite. After 50m turn right through a gate into a field. Keeping to the left-hand hedgerow for 200m to then walk on bearing about 240 degrees crossing a stile and on up the next field to exit through a gate to Dalwood Lane. Here turn right and after passing a residence walk up to Daneshill crossroads. Here turn left on a lane marked to 'Kilmington' and 'Axminster'.

In 100m bear right down a track, which soon becomes concreted. Just after where the concrete lane turns right, turn left down a track and into a small field. Cross the field exiting at the bottom right-hand corner, turning right and then left over a stile and planks over a ditch and into a small field. Exit the field in the bottom right-hand corner through a gate and into another field. Follow the right-hand hedgerow and after 60m turn right over a stile into the small neck of a field. Walk down the field exiting at the bottom through a gate and into another field. Walk alongside the left-hand hedgerow exiting at the bottom left through a gate to a lane by residences. Here turn right and go down to meet a lane on a bend, continue on in the same direction into Dalwood village.

Cross over the bridge over Corry Brook and in 20m turn right up a path. In 20m turn left round behind a building to arrive at a small car park. Cross the car park diagonally right to exit in front of a cottage and up to a gate. Go through the gate and into a field, the village church is on the left. Cross the field ahead to go over a footbridge and into another field. Maintain direction across the field slightly uphill, exiting over a stile and across another field. Exit through a gap in a hedgerow to walk across another field alongside the right-hand hedgerow. Exit in the top right-hand corner of the field through a gate to a lane (Ham Rd).

Cross the lane and go past a residence, go to the right of a hedgerow and on ahead. Then go left through the hedgerow and immediately turn right over a stile into a field. Cross the field slightly uphill to exit in the top right-hand corner through a gap in the hedgerow and into another field. Keeping to the right-hand hedgerow after 50m ignore footpath signs pointing left. Continue ahead to exit in the top right-hand corner into another field. Cross the field alongside the right-hand hedgerow exiting in the top right through a gate and into another field. Follow the right-hand hedgerow, bearing slightly right round to two gates about 30m apart. Ignore the first gate where a path leads off north. Go through the second gate on the left and up the field on the right-hand side on bearing about 260 degrees.

Walking parallel to overhead power cables in the field on the right, keep to the right-hand hedgerow to exit through a gate and on across another field slowly bearing right towards the overhead power cables. Once underneath the power cables at ST2281 0079 turn sharp left to cross the field away from the power cables on bearing about 250 degrees. Cross over a stile then go down steps and across a cross track to enter a field through a gate. Cross the field (Combehead Farm) keeping to the left-hand side to exit over a stile and into another field. Continue on ahead in the same direction across the field exiting over a stile to another field. Maintain direction to exit over a bar stile and a plank across a ditch to a lane by Lamb Farm.

Here turn right to walk along the grass verge soon pass under the power cables. After a further 700m and opposite Stockland Hill TV station, turn left down a lane. Follow the lane at times steeply downhill for 800m to a point where the lane turns sharp left by Hayne Farm (**Map 8**). Ignoring the first footpath sign through a gate on the right, turn right on the second footpath in a further 50m at the bend of the lane. Follow the track down to walk alongside the Umbourne Brook on the left. After 400m where the path joins close to the brook and by some steps going forward, turn left across the ford. (*To avoid crossing the ford at Umborne Brook go forward up the steps and continue alongside the brook for about 1km to a lane. Here turn left and after passing the village Church up to a T-junction. Turn left and after 750m arrive at Fourcross, to re-join the path, turn right*).

Follow the stony track uphill for 500m to pass Southcote Farm and onto a surfaced lane ahead. In a further 600m up to 'Fourcross'. Cross over the lane and continue up the track opposite. After 600m arrive at a lane (Cleverhayes Lane), here turn left along it. After 1km arrive at a junction where turn left on a road (Hutgate Rd) marked to 'Axminster'. Walk along the grass verge for 600m to a point opposite Northgate Lane.

Turn right down a track and in 25m go to the left of a gate. In 250m and just after passing underneath power cables turn left up steps and over a stile into a field. Cross the field immediately underneath the power cables and keeping to the right-hand hedgerow proceed into another field through a gap. Continue to contour across this hilly field to cross over two stiles by a gate in the bottom right-hand corner. Continue on in the same direction alongside the hedgerow then leaving the point of the hedgerow to cut across the field on bearing about 260 degrees to join a track to then bear right towards Hale Farm.

Walk through Hale Farm and then bear right down a track and in 50m, turn left through the middle of three gates. Go down a wide track and in 200m enter a field. Cross the field on the right-hand side and continue down to the bottom of the field where it becomes a lane by a residence. Go through a gate and proceed along Hale Lane and down to a T-junction with the A35(T). Turn right along it (Kings Rd) and go down to a roundabout where turn left. Walk along the High St and after 450m up to a T-junction with New St in Honiton.

Beaminster to Sherborne

Map: OS Explorer 116, 129
Start: The Square Beaminster
Finish: Sherborne Abbey
Distance: 37.3kms (23.0 miles)
Time: 9.25 hrs
Transport: Railway: Crewkerne, Yeovil Junction (800m north of Stoford), Sherborne
               Buses: Beaminster, Mosterton, Crewkerne (Haselbury Plucknett, East Coker, Barwick, Stoford, Bradford Abbas, all infrequent), Sherborne
Place of historical interest: Parnham House Beaminster, Sherborne Castle

The history

Prince William remained in Crewkerne during the day of the 25th November. It was here that Dr. Finch, Warden of All Souls College, Oxford was sent to Prince William assuring him that the heads of colleges would declare for him and inviting him to Oxford where 'their plate would be at his service'. With Bristol and Gloucester supporting William he had the whole West Country behind him – and now Oxford.

In Sherborne Prince William lodged in the castle, at the invitation of John Digby, third Earl of Bristol. It was here that the Third Declaration was read and distributed. The First declaration was dated the 10th October to which an additional one was added on the 24th October. The Third Declaration said:

'We have in the course of our whole Life, and more particularly by the apparent Hazards both by Sea and Land, to which we have so lately exposed our Person, given to the whole World so high and indoubted Proofs of our fervent Zeal for the Protestant Religion, that we are fully confident no true English-man and good Protestant can entertain the least Suspicion of our firm Resolution, rather to spend our dearest Blood and perish in the Attempt, than not to carry on the Blessed and Glorious Design which by the Favour of Heaven we have so successfully begun, to rescue England, Scotland and Ireland, from Slavery and Popery, and in a free Parliament to establish the Religion, the Laws and Liberties of those Kingdoms upon such a secure and lasting Foundation, that it shall not be in the Power of any Prince, for the future to introduce POPERY and TYRANNY.

Towards the more easie Compassing this great Design, we have not been hitherto deceived in the just Expectation we had of the Concurrence of the Nobility, Gentry and People of England, with Us for the Security of their Religion, the Restitution of the Laws, and the Re-establishment of their Liberties and Properties: Great Numbers of all Ranks and

Qualities have joined themselves to Us: and others at great Distances from Us, have taken up Arms and Declared for Us. And, which we cannot but particularly mention in that Army which was raised to be the Instrument of SLAVERY and POPERY, many (by the special Providence of God) both Officers and Common souldiers have been touched with such a feeling of sense of Religion and Honour, and of true Affection for their Native Country, that they have already deserted the Illegal Service they were engaged in, and have come over to Us, and have given us full Assurance from the rest of the Army, that they will certainly follow this Example, as soon as with our Army we shall approach near enough to receive them, without the Hazard of being prevented or betrayed. To which end, and that we may the sooner execute this just and necessary Design we are engaged in for the public Safety and Deliverance of these Nations, We are resolved with all possible Diligence to advance forward, that a Free Parliament maybe forthwith called, and such Parliament adjusted with the King, and all things first settled upon such a foot according to Law. As may give Us and the whole Nation just Reason to believe the King is disposed to make such necessary Condesentions on his part, as will give entire satisfaction and security to all, and make both King and People once more Happy. And that we may effect all this, in the way most agreeable to our Desires, if it be possible without the Effusion of any Blood except those execrable Criminals who have justly forfeited their Lives for betraying the Religion and Subverting the Laws of their Native Country. We do think fit to declare that as we will offer no Violence to any but in our own Necessary Defense: so we will not suffer any Injury to be done to the Person even a Papist, provided that he be found in such a Place, and in such Condition and Circumstances as the Law requires. So we are resolved and do declare that all Papists, who shall be found in open Arms, or with Arms in their Houses, or about their Persons or in any Office or Employment, civil or Military upon any pretense whatsoever contrary to the known Laws of the Land, shall be treated by Us and our Forces not as Souldiers and Gentlemen, but as Robbers, Free-Booters and Banditti: they shall be incapable of Quarter and entirely delivered up to the Discretion of our Souldiers. And We do further declare that all Persons who shall be found anyways aiding and assisting to them, or shall march under their Command, or shall joyn with or submit to them in the discharge or Execution of their Illegal Commissions or Authority, shall be looked upon as Partakers of their Crimes, Enemies to the Laws and to their Country.

And whereas we are certainly informed that Great Numbers of armed Papists have of late resorted to London and Westminster and parts adjacent, where they remain, as we have reason to suspect not so

*much for their own Security, as out of a wicked and barbarous Design
to make some desperate Attempt upon the said Cities, and their
Inhabitants by Fire, or a sudden Massacre, or both: or else to be the
more ready to joyn themselves to a Body of French Troops, designed if
it be possible, to land in England, procured by the French King, by the
Interest and Power of the Jesuits in Pursuance of their Engagements,
which at the Instigation of that Pestilent Society, his most Christian
Majesty with one of his Neighbouring Princes of the same
Communion has entered into for the utter Extirpation of the
Protestant Religion out of Europe. Though we hope we have taken
such effectual care to prevent the one, and secure the other, that by
god's Assistance, we cannot doubt but we shall defeat all their wicked
Enterprises and Designs. We cannot however fore bear out of the great
and tender concern. We have to preserve the People of England and in
particular those great and populous Cities, from the cruel Rage and
bloody Revenge of the Papists to Require and expect from all the Lord
Lieutenants, Deputy Lieutenants and the Justices of the Peace, Lord
Mayors, Mayors, Sheriffs, and all other Magistrates and Officers,
Civil and Military of all Counties, Cities and Towns of England,
especially of the County of Middlesex and Cities of London and
Westminster and Parts adjacent, that they do immediately disarm and
secure as by the Law they may and ought, within their respective
Counties, Cities and Jurisdictions, All Papists whatsoever as Persons at
all times, but now especially most dangerous to the Peace and Safety
of the Government, that so not only all Power of doing mischief may
be taken from them: but that the Laws, which are the greatest and best
Security may resume their Force, and be strictly Executed. And we do
hereby likewise Declare that We will Protect and Defend all those who
shall not be afraid to do their Duty in Obedience to these Laws. And
that for those Magistrates and others of what condition so ever they
be, who shall refuse to assist Us and in Obedience to the Laws to
Execute vigorously what we have require of them, and suffer
themselves at this Juncture to be cajoled or terrified out of their Duty.
We will esteem them the most Criminal and Infamous of all Men,
Betrayers of their Religion and Laws, and their Native Country, and
shall not fail to treat them accordingly: resolving to expect and require
at their hands the Life of every single Protestant that shall perish and
every House that shall burn or destroyed by their Treachery and
Cowardice.*

William Henry Prince of Orange
By His Highness special command
C Huygens
Sherborne 28 November 1688

The above was read and distributed from Sherborne, to the Protestants a rallying call, to the Catholics – junk mail.

It was claimed that Prince William knew nothing of it. It was probably written not by Prince William or his authorized advisors but by one Hugh Speke who apparently owned up to this forgery some years later. At the time of its publication its effect caught the feeling of the masses and was allowed to remain in circulation.

Whilst in Sherborne Prince William heard that Plymouth had declared their support for him, thereby also reducing the threat of a counter attack by the King from behind William's advancing army. Prince George of Denmark together with the Duke of Ormond joined William at Sherborne on the 29 November after their defections from James.

The route: Eastbound

Beaminster to Mosterton
6.0kms (3.75 miles) Time: 1.5 hrs

From The Square in Beaminster walk north along Fleet St for 800m to Newtown. At a Y-junction turn left up Chantry Lane. At its terminal point pass through Chantry Farm to join a track going uphill through a plantation, across a stream and over a stile. Turn half-left and go uphill soon bearing right to follow a narrow path rutted by cattle away from the valley and stream and up to a gate in the top right hand corner by a line of trees at ST4777 0301.

Go through the gate and on ahead on the right hand side of the field to exit through a gap and then a gate into another field. Here turn left and continue up the hill (Buckham Down) with a hedgerow on your left. Exit through a gate in the top of the field and into another field. Here go half-left to the top left-hand corner exiting through a gate to a lane. Cross the lane and walk along the lane/farm track opposite. In 600m where the lane/farm track swings left to North Buckham Farm at ST4760 0393 maintain the same direction on a track between hedgerows. Maintain this track for 900m exiting through a gate at a cross track at ST4740 0478.

Here turn left and into a field on bearing 260 degrees crossing to the left of farm buildings to exit through a gate in the left-hand corner of the field into another field. Cross the field half-left to exit through a gate into another field. Continue across the field to a gate and into another field. Continue on ahead to exit through a gate and over a footbridge to a field. Keeping to the right to exit through a gate into Baker's Mill Farm. Proceed in the same direction through several gates through the farm to exit into a field and on ahead on the right hand side of the field in the same direction. Exit through a gate to continue along a track between hedgerows. Pass farm buildings and onto a concrete track and up to a road A3066 at Mosterton. Here turn right along the road and into Mosterton village.

Mosterton to Crewkerne
5.5kms (3.5 miles) Time: 1.5 hrs

From Mosterton village walk north along the A3066 to turn left up Down Lane (**Map 13**). Keep on ahead for 1.5kms (1.0 miles) to where the lane turns sharp right at ST4475 0678. Here turn left down a track for 500m to a T-junction at Ducks' Field Crossing. Here turn right and in 200m turn left up a

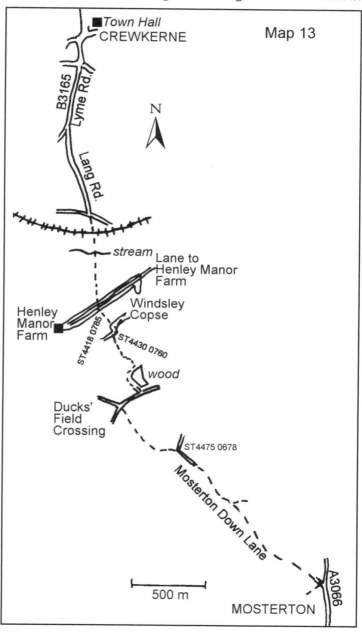

track and in 15m turn left over a stile into a field. Walk round the right-hand edge of the field and cross over a stile into a field. Cross the field on bearing about 340 degrees (*as per the waymark on top of the nearby post*) to arrive at a lane at ST4430 0760. Here turn right and go round an S-bend and turn left through the first gate on the left (*there is an adjacent stile*) into a field. Cross the field at about 320 degrees exiting through a gap to a lane at ST4418 0785.

Cross the lane and go down the track opposite in a wooded area then through a gate and into a field and on ahead on bearing due north 0 degrees. Exit over a stile and into a field, continue down the field to cross a

Town Hall, Crewkerne
Photo: L Ham

double stile and farm track and down to cross a stream over stepping-stones. Turn half-right uphill to cross a stile and into a field. Exit over a stile to cross a live railway line (*take care*) and a stile into another field. Continue on ahead to exit over a stile to a lane. Here turn left and in 10m at a T-junction turn right up Lang Rd and on to join Lyme Rd (B3165), here turn right and continue into Hermitage St. At a junction go forward into Market St and on into Market Square and up to the Town Hall in Crewkerne.

Crewkerne to Haselbury Plucknett
4.2kms (2.5 miles) Time: 1.0 hrs

From the Town Hall in Market Square walk east along East St (A30) and after 400m at Mount Pleasant bear right down a lane passing residences (Easthams Road) (**Map 14**). At its terminal point continue on ahead along a track to its terminal point to cross over a stile and into a field. Keeping to the left-hand edge to cross over a double stile and into another field. Exit over another stile into another field and on ahead. Contour the field to cross over a stile to a lane below Higher Easthams Farm. Here turn right and go down the lane. At the bottom by a residence continue on and go through a gate into a field.

Cross the field towards the footbridge, turning left before it, and up to a stile by a gate. Cross over it and a grassy bridge over the River Parrett and on ahead

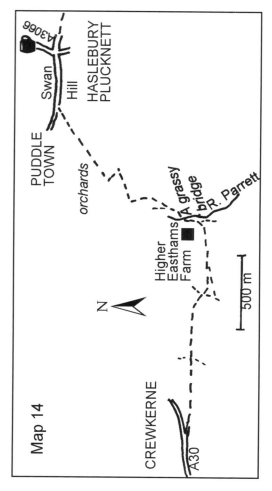

on a meandering path by the river. Exit over a stile built into a tree, here turn right and in 80m to a cross track (River Parrett Trail) where turn left. In about 100m go over a stile by a gate and take the path going up a hilly banking and in 100m in a line of trees, cross over a stile on the right into a field and go half-right across it.

Exit in the top right hand corner onto a track. After 250m on this track at the corner of an orchard find a white waymark and follow it and subsequent waymarks for 200m, and then turn left for 200m around the field (formerly an orchard) to a yellow waymark next to a metal stile on the right. Cross this stile and keep the hedge on your left. After 150m turn left over a stile in the hedgerow and into East Close. Here turn right and in 40m join a footpath by a row of bungalows, then exit to a road in Puddletown. Here turn right and on into Swan Hill and in 400m walk up to the A3066 in Haselbury Plucknett.

Haselbury Plucknett to East Coker
9.0kms (5.5 miles) Time: 2. 25 hrs

From the crossroads on the A3066 and Swan Hill, cross over the A3066 and continue on ahead along a lane. After 600m at a T-junction turn right and in a further 220m at a T-junction turn left. Follow the lane round to the right and at a T-junction turn left along New Rd and in 2.2kms (1.25 miles) to a T-junction at ST5015 1105 signposted to 'Hardington Marsh'. Here turn right and in 150m at a bend go on ahead on an unsurfaced lane passing commercial workings on the right. Where the lane ends go forward on a track between trees. Exit to a broad track between hedgerows and go forward up to Townsend Farm buildings (**Map 15**). Walk past the buildings and up to a T-junction. Here turn right and in 170m at a T-junction turn left into Hardington Mandeville.

At a T-junction maintain the same direction and in 200m arrive at the church of St Mary the Virgin. Go past the church and the village hall and at a junction of lanes turn right towards Hardington Moor. Where the lane turns left after 500m turn right through a gate by a residence and go up a track which soon enters a field. Here turn left keeping to the left-hand edge to exit over a stile in the left-hand corner and into another field. Bear left exiting over a stile in the bottom of the field and across a small field exiting through a gate to a lane. Here turn right and in 100m turn left over a stile into a field signposted to 'Primrose Hill and Penn Cross'. After 60m cross over a footbridge and into a field to go slightly right to join a hedgerow.

Walk alongside the hedgerow exiting through a gate into another field where turn half-left across the field, exiting over a stile in the middle of a hedgerow and onto a path by a fenced wild life breeding sanctuary. Go forward up to a gate at a lane by 'Merry Moles', a residence, here turn right and in 100m before 'Haygrove', a residence, turn left on a track signposted to 'Lodge Hill'. Follow the track, which becomes a lane passing Westfield Farm and up to a lane at a T-junction. Cross over the lane and go through a gate opposite and into a field and on ahead between lines of trees. Exit through a gate by a residence and walk up to a lane at a bend. Continue on ahead in the same direction. In 200m at a T-junction turn left and continue onto a track ahead and down to a lane passing by a millennium commemorative stone. Walk along the lane in the same direction and in 180m arrive at a T-junction on your right at ST5388 1288 in East Coker.

East Coker to Bradford Abbas
6.6kms (4.0 miles) Time: 1.5 hrs

See special note on page 79

From the T-junction at ST5388 1288 in East Coker (**Map 16**) walk east along the lane for 50m and turn left over a stile and into a field crossing it on bearing about 60 degrees to the top right hand corner to a junction of 6 paths. Cross over a stile into a small field following a path marked 'Pavyotts Mill' on general bearing of about 70 degrees. In 25m cross over a second stile and in a further 25m cross over a third stile into another field and along by the side of a stream. Exit over a stile and into another field and on ahead. Exit over a double stile into another field. Exit over a stile by a line of trees and cross several stiles following the stream for about 600m to a footbridge on the left.

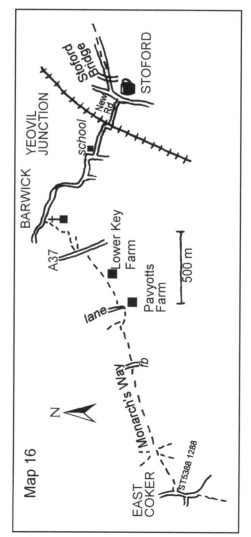

Cross the footbridge, then turn right and continue with the stream on your right to Pavyotts Mill in another 400m, exiting through a gate to a lane. Here turn left and in 50m turn right over a stile into a field. Cross the field on bearing about 60 degrees to continue past Lower Key farm to exit over a stile to the A37. Here turn left and in 15m cross over the road and go up the banking to go over steps over a fence and into a field. Here turn left and follow the edge of the field round to the top left hand corner exiting over a stile into a small field. Exit over another stile into another small field. Then go through a gate and onto a footpath to go through another gate and onto a track and up to a lane by St Mary Magdalene C of E church in Barwick.

Here turn right and follow the lane round to the right for 400m ignoring other lanes and up to a T-junction by a school. Go on ahead up Southview and at a T-junction where turn left into Higher Bullen. Walk down to a T-junction where turn left under a railway bridge and on

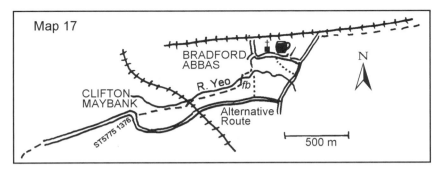

into Stoford along New Rd. At a T-junction turn left and in 50m at a T-junction turn right along a lane soon crossing Stoford Bridge. After 1.1kms (0.75 miles) at Clifton Maybank (**Map 17**) just after the lane has turned right, turn left through a gate and into a field at ST5775 1376. Cross the field on bearing about 80 degrees to walk alongside the River Yeo. Exit the field through a gate and then go underneath a railway arch to exit through a gate and into another field. **(See special note below)** Follow the course of the river to exit over a footbridge after 500m. Go up an enclosed path to join a track where turn right. The track continues as Mill Lane and up to a T-junction at Church Rd. Continue forward and up to St Mary the Virgin Church in Bradford Abbas.

> *Special Note: At the time of writing, the footbridge over the River Yeo is in need of repair forcing its closure. Meanwhile an alternative route round the problem is as follows:*
>
> *200m before the footbridge bear right across the field to exit over a stile to a lane. Here turn left and in 400m go up to a T-junction where turn left. In 200m just after crossing Smith's Bridge turn left through a gate and into a field. Cross the field keeping to the right to exit through a gate onto a footpath and up to Church Rd. Here turn left and walk up to St Mary the Virgin Church in Bradford Abbas.*

Bradford Abbas to Sherborne
6.0kms (3.75 miles) Time: 1.5 hrs

From the church St Mary the Virgin walk east along Church St for 375m to its terminal point at a T-junction. Here turn left and in 250m before a railway bridge turn right through a gate into a field. Continue alongside the railway line to go through a gate into another field exiting through a gate by a cottage at a railway crossing. Turn left and cross over the active railway lines (*take care*) and turn right to pass farm buildings and on up to a T-junction. Cross over the junction to go through a gate into a field exiting through a line of trees and into another field. Cross the field on bearing about 60 degrees to exit over two stiles by Keepers Cottage and into a field.

Skirt round the cottage and continue on ahead in the same direction along the left-hand edge of the field to go through a gap and into another field. Exit over a stile and into another field and on ahead alongside a hedgerow. Where the hedgerow swings lefts at its protruding point carry on ahead and up to

Silverlake Farm to cross over a stile to the right of the farm buildings and into a field. Cross the field (Lenthay Common) on bearing about 80 degrees to join a hedgerow after 700m and in a further 100m to exit over a stile to a track. Here turn right and in 50m at a T-junction turn left on a track. When the track becomes a road (Lenthay Rd) carry on ahead and up to a road junction (A352). Cross over the A352 and continue into Horsecastles and at a crossroads cross over into Trendle St then into Half Moon St and up to Sherborne Abbey.

The route: Westbound

Sherborne to Bradford Abbas
6.0kms (3.75 miles) Time: 1.5 hrs

From Sherborne Abbey walk west along Half Moon St and into Trendle St and on into Horsecastles. At a road junction with the A352 cross over the road and proceed along Lenthay Rd. At its terminal point by Sherborne Abbey Primary School continue on ahead along a track. At a T-junction turn right and in 50m turn left over a stile and into a field. Cross the field (Lenthay Common) on bearing about 260 degrees aiming to the left of Silverlake Farm buildings after 800m (*the farm buildings cannot be seen until you are halfway across the field*). Ignore a stile on the right into the farm garden and exit over a stile to another field crossing it on bearing about 235 degrees. In 150m join the protruding point of a hedgerow then walk alongside it. (the hedgerow on your right)

Exiting over a stile to another field continue ahead along the right-hand edge and into another field through a gap. Walk on to the right-hand corner to go left

Riders passing the Rose and Crown, Bradford Abbas

Photo: L Ham

Sherborne Abbey

Photo: L Ham

round Keepers Cottage exiting over a double stile and into another field. Maintain the same direction to go through a line of trees and into another field and on ahead parallel with the railway. Exit through a gate to a T-junction of lanes at a farm. Continue forward past farm buildings and after 120m turn left through a gate to cross over an active railway line (*take care*). Having crossed the railway line turn immediately right through a gate and kissing gate ahead into a field (**Map 17**). Keeping to the right-hand edge of the field to exit through a gate and on into another field. Exit through a gate to a lane where turn left and in 250m turn right along Church Rd and arrive at the church of St Mary the Virgin in Bradford Abbas.

Bradford Abbas to East Coker
6.6kms (4.0 miles) Time: 1.5 hrs

See special note on page 82

From the church of St Mary the Virgin walk westbound along Church Rd. At a bend turn left down Mill Lane to its end and then continue along a track. At a gate turn left before it down an enclosed path to cross a footbridge over the River Yeo and into a field. Turn right to follow the course of the river (**detour rejoins here**) exiting through a gate to go under a railway arch. Exit through a gate and into a field. Walk alongside the river and then continue the line across the field on bearing about 260 degrees to exit through a gate and to a lane at Clifton Maybank. Here turn right.

> **Special Note:** *At the time of writing the footbridge over the River Yeo is in need of repair forcing its closure. Meanwhile an alternative route round the problem is as follows:*
>
> *From St Mary the Virgin church walk east back along Church Rd and opposite the Post Office turn right on a footpath and then go through a gate into a field. Follow the footpath round to the left and in 200m exit through a gate to a lane. Here turn right crossing Smith's Bridge and in 150m at a T-junction turn right along the road to Clifton Maybank and Stoford. Walk along this road and in 400m turn right over a stile and into a field. Cross the field and walk up to the River Yeo (to join the path from the footbridge), here turn left to continue as marked in the previous paragraph.*

Continue along the road for a further 1.1kms (0.75 miles) crossing Stoford Bridge (**Map 16**) and up to a T-junction at Stoford. Here turn left and in 50m at a T-junction turn right along New Rd. Immediately after going underneath a railway bridge turn right into Higher Bullen and up to a T-junction. Here turn right down Southview and to a T-junction by a school. Go on ahead in the same direction following the road round to the right to Barwick. Just after St Mary Magdalene C of E church on the left turn left up a track then immediately right through a gate to a footpath, then immediately through a gate to cross a small field. Cross over a stile and another small field exiting in the top right-hand corner to another field. Here turn right and follow the edge of the field to the corner and then turn left along the hedgerow parallel to the road (A37).

In 100m cross over the fence by way of steps and go down a slope to the road (A37). Cross over the road and turn left and in 15m turn right on a path marked 'Pavyotts Mill', go over a stile and into a field. In 100m cross a track and enter another field and continue on bearing 235 degrees to exit over a stile in a hedgerow to a lane at Pavyotts Mill. Here turn left, and in 40m, turn right through a gate along a path. In 60m go through a gate and on ahead on a path marked 'Moor Lane'. In a further 100m go through a gate and in 15m go through a second gate and into a field. Keeping to the left-hand edge of the field by a stream, in 300m turn left over a footbridge over a stream and into a field.

Turn right to follow the stream and going over several stiles and fields arrive at a distinctive six-directional footpath signpost. Here turn half-left on bearing of 230 degrees (still following the stream) to exit over a stile in the right-hand corner to a track. Turn right on the track to a T-junction at a lane in East Coker at ST5388 1288 (**Map 15**).

East Coker to Haselbury Plucknett
9.0kms (5.5 miles) Time: 2.25 hrs

At the T-junction turn left and in 180m at a millennium commemorative stone, bear right up a path marked 'Back St'. The track becomes a lane, continue on up to a T-junction, and here turn right. Where the lane turns left continue on ahead through a gate by a residence. Proceed ahead between lines of trees exiting through a gate to a lane at a T-junction. Take the lane ahead past Westfield Farm and where the surfaced lane ends onto a track at a Y-junction take the left-hand track. Continue up to a T-junction at a lane by a residence 'Haygrove' and here turn right.

In 130m by a residence, 'Merry Moles', turn left down a path marked 'Penn Cross'. At the bottom of the track cross over a stile and into a field. Cross the field and ignoring the stile ahead go half-right to the bottom right-hand corner exiting through a gate into a field, then keep to the left-hand side of the field alongside a hedgerow. At the end of the hedgerow continue on ahead to cross a footbridge over a stream then cross a small field on the left-hand side exiting over a stile to a lane. Here turn right and in 100m turn left through a gate into a small field exiting in the top right-hand corner over a stile into another field. Here go half-right for 60m to exit over a stile in the hedgerow to another field.

Continue on ahead on the right-hand edge and at the end of the hedgerow join a track. Bearing right go down to a gate by a cottage and down to a lane. Here turn left and in 500m at a road junction turn left into Hardington Mandeville past the village hall and up to the church of St Mary the Virgin. Continue on through the village and after 200m at a T-junction continue on ahead in the same direction on a lane marked 'Pendomer 2 miles'. At a T-junction turn right and after 150m turn left down a lane soon to walk through Townsend Farm. Carry on down a broad grassy track between hedgerows on a bearing of about 250 degrees.

Where the track swings left go through a rather flimsy gate and maintain same direction on a narrower path between trees exiting to a track. After passing commercial workings on the left arrive at a lane at a bend. Continue forward in the same direction and up to a T-junction. Here turn left along New Rd and follow the road signs to Haselbury Plucknett. In 2.3kms (1.5 miles) at a T-junction turn right. In 250m at a T-junction turn right. In 200m at a T-junction turn left. After 600m arrive at the A3066 at Haselbury Plucknett.

Haselbury Plucknett to Crewkerne
4.2kms (2.5 miles) Time: 1.0 hrs

From the A3066 in Haselbury Plucknett (**Map 14**) cross over the road and walk along Swan Hill and in 400m at Puddletown turn left along a footpath marked 'Crewkerne' 2 miles and 'River Parrett' 1 mile. Go past cottages and up to a road East Close. In 40m turn left over a stile and into a field. Immediately turn right and exit in the right-hand corner over a stile. Turn left for 200m to a pole with a white waymark. Turn right and follow the track for 500m passing lines of windbreak trees, which formerly sheltered orchards to a small field, crossing slightly right to exit over a stile in 60m. Here turn left down the side of a hill to cross over a stile and briefly join a track, the 'River Parrett Trail'. In about 100m veer right to cross over a stile built into a tree beside the River Parrett. Follow the meandering path to exit over a grassy bridge then a stile and into a field.

Proceed ahead to a footbridge on the left (*do not cross*), here turn right uphill across the field and go through a gate by a residence and on up to a lane. At a right-hand bend turn left over a stile and into a field. Contour the field on initial bearing 270 degrees slowly veering right to cross over a stile into another field and on ahead. Exit over a double stile keeping to the right hand edge and exiting over a stile to a track. Proceed on ahead between hedgerows ignoring other paths and up to a lane with residences and on up to the A30. Here turn left and then along East St continuing on into Market Square and up to the Town Hall in Crewkerne.

Crewkerne to Mosterton
5.5kms (3.5 miles) Time 1.5 hrs

From the Town Hall in Market Square (**Map 13**) walk west into Market St and then into Hermitage St (B3165) and in 500m into Lyme Rd. In 40m turn left into Lang Rd and continue to its terminal point in 700m at a T-junction. Here turn left and in 10m turn right over a stile into a field. Continue on ahead exiting over a stile to cross an active single-track railway line (*take care*) and over another stile into a field. Maintain same direction to exit over a stile and then turn right down a slope to cross over a stream on stepping-stones and up to a farm track. Cross over the track and go over a double stile and into a field and on ahead up the hill in the same direction.

Exit over a stile, then go on ahead exiting through a gate and onto a track. In 40m go up to a lane at ST4418 0785. Cross over the lane and enter a field opposite and on ahead in the same direction exiting through a gate to a lane at an S-bend at ST4432 0765. Here turn right and in 100m turn left over a stile and into a field. Cross the field on a bearing of 170 degrees aiming for the right-hand edge of a copse to exit over a stile into a field.

Follow the field round to the left under power lines exiting in the bottom left-hand corner over a stile. Here turn right and in 15m go up to a lane at ST4450 0719. Here turn right and in 200m at a T-junction turn left up a track signposted 'Sandy Lane to Knowle Lane'. In 500m arrive at a lane on a bend, continue on in the same direction and after 1.5kms (1.0 miles) walk up to a road (A3066) at Mosterton.

Mosterton to Beaminster
6.0kms (3.75 miles) Time: 1.5 hrs

From Down Lane and the A3066 turn right and go through Mosterton and in 600m turn left on a concrete track marked 'Buckham Down 3 miles'. Continue past farm buildings and onto a track between hedgerows. Exit through a gate into a field and on ahead. Exit through a gate to go through Baker's Mill Farm. At the farm buildings go through several gates and on ahead in the same direction on the left-hand side of a field. Exit through a gate and over a footbridge and into another field.

Cross the field exiting through a gate to cross a second field. Exit through a gate to go half-left across another field keeping to the right of farm buildings. Exit through a gate to cross a field aiming to go through a gap in a line of trees and to a cross track at ST4740 0479. Here turn right through a gate to proceed on a track amongst trees for 900m, then join a farm track where turn left, in a further 600m, and walk up to a lane. Cross over the lane and go through a gate to go slightly left exiting through a gate into another field (Buckham Down). Walk down the field on the right hand side exiting in the right-hand corner to another field. Then carry on down the left-hand side of the field to exit through a gate in the left-hand corner at ST4777 0301.

Walk down and across an irregular field bearing slightly right between bushes to exit in the bottom left-hand corner to a stile by a gate. Cross over the stile and over a stream following the path left and through a plantation and down to Chantry Farm. Go past the farm buildings to join Chantry Lane ahead and down to a T-junction at Newtown. Here turn right and then along Fleet St and up to The Square at Beaminster.

Sherborne to Wincanton

Map: OS Explorer 129
Start: Sherborne Abbey
Finish: High St, Wincanton
Distance: 30.1kms (18.5 miles)
Time: 7.5 hrs
Transport: Railway: Sherborne, Templecombe (1.6kms (1.0 miles)
north of Yenston)
   Buses: Sherborne, (Yenston, Kington Magna, Buckhorn
Weston, Cucklington, all infrequent), Wincanton
Place of historical interest: Sherborne Castle, The Dogs South St Wincanton
(private residence)

Special Note: On this section between Sherborne and Wincanton refreshments are only available in Buckhorn Weston, village shops or Stapleton Arms, which is 21.9kms (13.5 miles) from Sherborne and 8.0kms (5.0 miles) from Wincanton. This section crosses Blackmore Vale and is prone to flooding but a considerable portion of the walk is on pleasant country lanes.

The history

The vanguard of William's army had reached Wincanton whilst William was still in Exeter and it was at Wincanton that the first blood of the Revolution had been spilled earlier. Contemporary reports tell of a skirmish that took place, about fifteen soldiers were buried in a communal grave – the first blood in action, of this 'bloodless revolution'. A report received by the Revd Whittle from Mr Webb a Cornet of Horse as follows:

A Lieutenant having his Post at this Town, with about four and twenty Souldiers belonging to the Regiment of the Honourable Major General Mackay, hearing that a party of Horse belonging to King James were posting thither, he was so magnanimous as to resolve to fight them; and in order thereto, posted his men as securely as he could, in a small Inclosure, at the East end of the Town, on the left side; there was a good hedg between them and the Road, which was to defend them against the horse, and through which they were to fire upon the Enemy; but there was a little Gate at one Corner, and a weak dead Hedg. In this Field he posted most of his Men; and on the other side of the way. Just opposite to this place, he posted about six Souldiers in a little Garden, who had a thick Hedg to cover them from the Horse, and through which they were to fire. The Officer himself, with four or five Men, keeping the Road. The Enemies horse being now advanced within Musquet-shot, the Souldiers would have fired upon them; but the Lieutenant, whose name was Cambel, not knowing what they might be; whether Friends or foes, would not permit them, and the more, because a Regiment of Horse belonging to my Lord Cornbury, was come in and joined our Forces, and so advancing each towards other, our Officer first gave them the Word, saying, Stand, Stand, For who are ye? To which the Enemies Officer, at the Head of the Party of Horse, answered, I am for King James, who art thou for? To which our Officer replied, I am for the Prince of Orange.

God damn me, says the Enemies Officer, I will Prince thee. Whereupon our officer said, Fire; and went boldly up to this Popish officer and shot him in at his Mouth and through his Brains, so he drop'd down dead; our Souldiers firing upon them through the Hedges on each side, maul'd them desperately, and killed several of them. They carried off their Dead presently, being ten to one (for the Enemies Party was about one hundred and fifty, and our party but five and twenty.) The rode to find a Place to break in upon our Men; so some Horse broke in at the upper end of the Croft, some at the lower Corner, and others got in at the little Gate, which, as is said, was open'd by a Townsman that stood near the Place, so that our Men charged as fast as they could to fire upon them, but were now surrounded with the Enemy; our souldiers were divers of them kill'd. They defended themselves as well as 'twas possible, for such a handful against so many; and one or two of them being shot in five or six places, were offer'd Quarter by the Enemy for their great Courage, but they would not accept of it from the Hands of Papists, and therefore chose rather to die.

Now the little Company in the Garden fired divers times, and the Officer, with his Men, kept their ground awhile, and then got into the Garden to their own Party. The Towns-people were much alarmed by this Action, and came thronging into the Streets; and kind Providence having so ordain'd it, for the Saving of our Men (else, no doubt, they would all have been cut off, being so mightily overpowerd) that a certain Miller came riding in at the other end of the Town, and hearing of this Skirmish, presently reported, that he had overtaken a strong party of Horse belonging to the Prince of Orange, and that he believed that they were now entring the Town; This was brought to the Enemies Ears very quickly, and moreover he call'd to them, and said, Away, for your Lives, save your selves, the Enemies are at hand. Now these Souldiers of the late King James, seeing the People of the Town so thick in the Streets, running here and there, judged that it might be so, and hereupon they retreated with all speed, galloping away in a confused manner; however, they left more behind kill'd on their side, than they had kill'd of our Men, for 'twas the Judgement of all here that this handful of Souldiers (appertaining to his Highness the Prince of Orange) kill'd more of their Enemies than they themselves were in number.

There were about fifteen tumbled in one Grave together, and about eight or nine of our men, the rest being of the Enemies Party. Our Officers did most of them visit this Mr Webb, cornet of horse, to hear the manner of this small Action'

Whilst in Wincanton it is said William lodged at the house of a Mr Churchey, at The Dogs in South St.

This section contains a few kilometres of interesting winding lane walking which reminded me of the following poem:

The Rolling English Road

Before the Roman came to Rye or out to Severn stode,
The rolling English drunkard made the rolling English road
A reeling road, a rolling road, that rambles round the shire,
And after him the parson ran, the sexton and the squire;
A merry road, a mazy road, and such as we did tread
The night we went to Birmingham by way of Beachy Head.

I knew no harm of Bonapart and plenty of the Squire,
And for to fight the Frenchman I did not much desire;
But I did bash their baggonets because they came array'd
To straighten out the crooked road an English drunkard made,
Where you and I went down the lane with ale-mugs in our hands,
The night we went to Glastonbury by way of Goodwin Sands.

His sins they were forgiven him; or why do flowers run
Behind him; and the hedges all strengthening in the sun?
The wild thing went from left to right and knew not which was which,
But the wild rose was above him when they found him in the ditch.
God pardon us, nor harden us; we did not see so clear
The night we went to Bannockburn by way of Brighton Pier.

My friends we will not go again or ape an ancient rage,
Or stretch the folly of our youth to be the shame of age,
But walk with clearer eyes and ears this path that wandereth,
And see undrugg'd in evening light the decent inn of death;
For there is good news yet to hear and fine things to be seen,
Before we go to Paradise by way of Kensal Green.

G K Chesterton

The route: Eastbound

Sherborne to Goathill
5.0kms (3.0 miles) Time: 1.25 hrs

From Sherborne Abbey walk east along Half Moon St and turn right into South St. At a junction before the railway station go left to cross over the railway crossing and up Gas House Hill to a T-junction (New Rd). Cross over the road and go through a gate and turn left to walk up the side of the hill. Go through a gate and on ahead with Sherborne Castle on your left. Proceed ahead on the main track for 1.6kms (1.0 miles) and up to a gate by a lodge at a wood.

Carry on up the hill and round to the right to go through a gate and into a wood. Press on through the wood ignoring tracks to left or right and up to 'The Camp' and a collection of storage buildings. Here turn right along a road. At a junction of roads continue ahead in the same direction to exit through ornate gates by a lodge and up to a junction of lanes at ST6700 1583. Here turn left and in 1.3kms (0.75 miles) up to a T-junction (Goathill Rd) south of Goathill village at ST6773 1677. (This junction has a signpost with a grid reference of 677167).

Goathill to Crendle Corner
2.1kms (1.25 miles) Time: 0.5 hrs

From the T-junction at Goathill Rd turn right and in 30m turn left into Hanover Wood. Follow the path ahead to join a path to go round the edge of a protected area, first turning left then in 40m turning right. Initially take a bearing of 50 degrees but always following the footpath signs and in 1.7kms (1.0 miles) cross over a footbridge to enter a field. Cross the field half-right and in 50m go into another field passing a ditch and in 50m go through a gate to a road (A30) at Crendle Corner at ST6890 1814. Turn right along the A30 for 50m then cross over the road to T-junction opposite by a residence.

Crendle Corner to Yenston
6.2kms (3.75 miles) Time: 1.5 hrs

From the T-junction on the A30 walk in a northerly direction away from the A30 along a private drive by a residence and in 100m turn left on a footpath into Crendle Hill Wood. Follow the track uphill, keeping the fence of the field on the right in view, soon going round to the right to join a narrow footpath on bearing 320/330 degrees. In 500m exiting through a gate to join a wider track. Continue on ahead in the same direction to exit at a gate to a cross track at ST6870 1880, here turn right. Follow this track ahead to join a surfaced lane (The Old Road) after 600m, and in a further 1km just before the road joins the A30 turn left up a footpath, signposted to 'Bowden Lane 1 mile' and through a gate and into a field.

Keeping to the left of the field walk up Toomer Hill alongside the edge of a wood and in the top left-hand corner turn left through a gap in the hedgerow. Then turn immediately right, to skirt along the top edge of two fields and onto a track and up to Bowden Lane at ST6973 2024. Here turn sharp right and in

700m where the lane turns sharp right go through a gate ahead and into a field. Cross the field on bearing about 50 degrees exiting through a gate and into another field and then through another gate into a third field. Carry on ahead and onto a track down through trees exiting over a stile and in 100m to join a track at a T-junction. Here turn right along a track and on ahead to Chapel Lane and into Yenston at a T-junction with the A357.

Yenston to Kington Magna
6.8kms (4.25 miles)
Time: 1.75 hrs

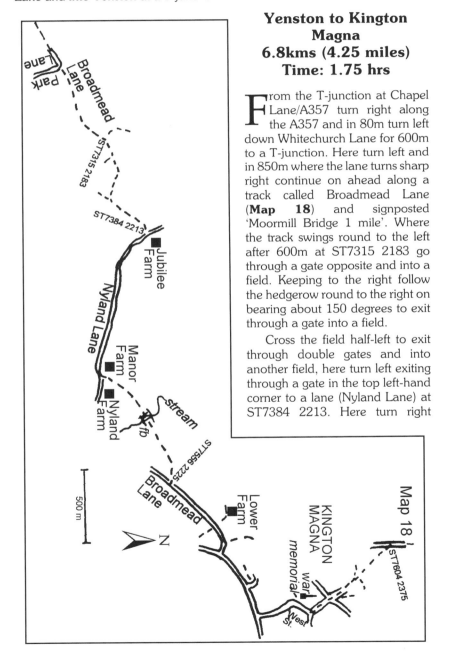

From the T-junction at Chapel Lane/A357 turn right along the A357 and in 80m turn left down Whitechurch Lane for 600m to a T-junction. Here turn left and in 850m where the lane turns sharp right continue on ahead along a track called Broadmead Lane (**Map 18**) and signposted 'Moormill Bridge 1 mile'. Where the track swings round to the left after 600m at ST7315 2183 go through a gate opposite and into a field. Keeping to the right follow the hedgerow round to the right on bearing about 150 degrees to exit through a gate into a field.

Cross the field half-left to exit through double gates and into another field, here turn left exiting through a gate in the top left-hand corner to a lane (Nyland Lane) at ST7384 2213. Here turn right along the lane for 1.1kms (0.75 miles) and turn left by the entrance to Manor Farm but before Nyland Farm. Go through a gate and into a field, continue down the right hand edge for 200m and go through a gate on the right into another field. Here turn left to walk down the other side of the hedgerow to a gate in the bottom left hand corner.

Go through the gate and cross the field half-right to a metal footbridge over a stream. Cross over it into a field and go half-left to a gate and into another field. Cross the field half-right to exit through a gate and onto a track also called Broadmead Lane at ST7556 2225. Here turn left and in 500m proceed onto a surfaced lane at Lower Farm and on up to a T-junction at a lane. Here turn left into Kington Magna. At a T-junction keep on ahead and in 200m at a junction turn left into West St. Follow the road round and after 300m arrive at the war memorial on the left at Kington Magna.

Kington Magna to Wincanton
10.0kms (6.25 miles) Time: 2.5 hrs

Walk on past the war memorial for 50m to a T-junction where turn left. At a crossroads continue on ahead along a lane to its end then turn right through a gate on a footpath along the edge of a field by a fence. At the bottom of the field turn right over a stile and immediately left and in 5m go through two gates and into a field. Cross the field on bearing 320 degrees exiting in the left-hand corner to a lane at ST7604 2375 (Map 18).

Here turn right and in 800m go under a railway arch and into Buckhorn Weston. At a T-junction continue on ahead for 2.6kms (1.5 miles) ignoring other lanes to go along Shave Hill and Weyclose Lane and up to a T-junction. Here turn left into Cucklington. Follow the lane out of Cucklington towards Stoke Trister and after 1.6kms (1.0 miles) at a T-junction turn left along Shaftesbury Lane for 2.4kms (1.5 miles) to a T-junction where turn right into Wincanton along Common Rd and up to the High St at Wincanton.

The route: Westbound

| See Section 6 Special Note on page 85 |

Wincanton to Kington Magna
10.0kms (6.25 miles) Time: 2.5 hrs

From High St/Common Rd at Wincanton walk down Common Rd to cross overhead the A303 (T). At a T-junction after 200m turn left along a lane (Shaftesbury Lane) to Cucklington. After 2.4kms (1.5 miles) at a T-junction turn right and after 1.6kms (1.0 miles) into Cucklington maintaining the higher level road. Leaving Cucklington arrive at a T-junction after about 600m. Here turn right and ignoring other lanes continue on Weyclose Lane then Shave Hill to Buckhorn Weston after 2.6kms (1.5 miles). At a T-junction continue on ahead under a railway arch.

After 400m at a T-junction proceed in the same direction and in a further 400m just past residences turn left over a stile at ST7604 2375 (**Map 18**). Cross the field on bearing about 140 degrees. Exit through double gates into a field and in 5m turn right over a stile then left to follow the fence up to a lane. Here turn left and after crossing a crossroads arrive at a T-junction in Kington Magna. Here turn right and up to the war memorial on the right.

Kington Magna to Yenston
6.8kms (4.25 miles) Time: 1.75 hrs

From the war memorial in Kington Magna walk south west to join West St and walk through the village to a junction of lanes. Here turn right and onto a T-junction where go straight ahead on a lane signposted to 'Yeovil and Shaftesbury'. After 300m turn right up a lane towards Lower Farm and where the lane turns right into the farm continue on ahead on a track (Broadmead Lane).

After 450m at ST7556 2225 turn right through a gate into a field crossing slightly left to go through another gate into a field crossing to the left again to a metal footbridge. Cross over the footbridge and go half-left exiting through a gate into a field then keeping to the right hand hedgerow walk up to a gate on the right. Go through the gate and turn left to continue along the line of the hedgerow now on your left, as is Nyland Farm and stables. Exit through a gate in the left-hand corner and up to a lane by the entrance to Manor Farm.

Here turn right along the lane for 1.1kms (0.75 miles) and just past Jubilee Farm at ST7384 2213 turn left through a gate into a field. Cross the field to the bottom right hand corner and go through two gates into another field. Cross the field half-left to exit through the right hand of two gates and on into another field. Cross the field on bearing about 330 degrees following the hedgerow round to the left to then go on bearing about 250 degrees to the left-hand corner of the field exiting through a gate at ST7315 2183.

Here walk ahead on a track (another Broadmead Lane) and after 600m to join a lane (Park Lane) at a bend. Proceed in the same direction and in 850m arrive at a T-junction. Here turn right onto Whitechurch Lane and in a further 600m proceed up to a T-junction with the A357. Here turn right and in 80m turn left into Chapel Lane.

Yenston to Crendle Corner
6.2kms (3.75 miles) Time: 1.5 hrs

From Chapel Lane T-junction with the A357. Walk along Chapel Lane to its end then ahead on a track. In 400m at a Y-junction turn left down a track and in 100m go over a stile and on ahead up to a field with a wooded area on the left exiting through a gate into another field. Then on ahead on bearing about 240 degrees through another gate into another field exiting through a gate onto a lane (Bowden Lane) on a bend at ST7035 2070. Go ahead in the same direction for 700m to ST6973 2024 where turn sharp left onto a track, signposted 'A30 and Stalbridge'. Walk along the track on bearing about 150 degrees to cross the top of two fields and into a wooded area. At a gate turn left before it through a gap and into a field.

Here turn right and keeping to the right hand edge of the field walking alongside the wood for 700m down Toomer Hill exiting through a gate to a lane. Here turn right along the lane (The Old Road) for 1.1kms (0.75 miles). Where the lane turns right into Gospel Ash Farm walk ahead along a track for

600m to a cross track at ST6870 1880. Here turn left down through Crendle Hill Wood to go through a gate and onto a narrower path and on ahead keeping to the left-hand edge of the wood by a field. At the end of the field follow the track round to the left exiting the wood at a lane, here turn right and walk down to the A30 by Crendle Corner.

Crendle Corner to Goathill
2.1kms (1.25 miles) Time: 0.5 hrs

A t the A30 turn right along it for 50m to go left through a gate and across a field half-left by a line of trees and a ditch and in another 50m up to a gate and footbridge. Cross the footbridge and enter Hanover Wood following bridleway signs for 1.7kms (1.0 miles). Then go left, then right, round a protected plantation exiting the wood to a lane (Goathill Rd) at ST6773 1677. Here turn right and in 30m up to a T-junction. (*A sign gives the grid reference here as 677167*).

Goathill to Sherborne
5.0kms (3.0 miles) Time: 1.25 hrs

F rom the T-junction walk along the lane to Haydon on bearing about 220 degrees and after 1.3kms (0.75 miles) at a junction at ST6700 1583 turn right through ornate gates by a lodge. (*The right of way to Sherborne is waymarked*) Follow the surfaced road bearing round to the left into a wood and after 600m up to 'The Camp' and a collection of storage buildings. Once up to the buildings turn left onto a track before the last building on the left and into a wooded area ignoring paths to left or right. Exit through a gate into a field to bear round to the left and downhill to a lodge and on ahead through a gate onto a track.

After 1.1kms (0.75 miles) where the track goes right towards Sherborne Castle take the path ahead through a gate in the same direction and up a hill. Exit through a gate to bear left on a path and descend alongside a road (New Rd) and down to a gate at a T-junction. Exit through a gate and cross the road and go down Gas House Hill to cross over a railway crossing and on ahead into South St. Turn left into Half Moon St and up to Sherborne Abbey.

Section 7

Wincanton to Hindon

Map: OS Explorer 129, 142, 143
Start: High St/ Ireson Lane crossroads at Wincanton
Finish: High St/The Dene crossroads at Hindon
Distance: 24.3kms (15.0 miles)
Time: 6.25 hrs
Transport: Railway: None nearby
                        Buses: Wincanton, Zeals, Mere, Hindon
Place of historical interest: The Dogs South St Wincanton (private residence)

The history

It is said of Hindon that its greatest occasion in its history was probably in 1688 when the Earl of Clarendon met William of Orange there.

The route: Eastbound

Wincanton to Zeals
9.3kms (5.75 miles) Time: 2.5 hrs

From the junction of High St and Ireson Lane in Wincanton go up Ireson Lane and then into Grants Lane to its terminal point. Go to the right of Windmill Farmhouse and along a path behind residences signed to 'Bayford' and 'Charlton Musgrove'. At the end of the residences go over a stile and into a field keeping to the left. In 50m at the end of a hedgerow go half-left across the field to exit in a narrow neck of the field over a stile by a gate. Keep to the left-hand edge exiting in the bottom left hand corner over a stile by a gate.

In 40m cross a track then go over a stile into a field. Continue down the field exiting in the bottom left hand corner to cross a footbridge over a stream and into another field. Continue on ahead across the field exiting over two stiles and another footbridge to another field. Cross the field at about 40 degrees exiting over a stile into another field. Continue on ahead crossing over two fields by stiles to exit over a stile to a lane (Rectory Lane) (**Map 19**). Here turn right and in 600m immediately past The Coach House turn right over a stile into a field, signposted 'Southmarsh half a mile'.

Cross the field on bearing about 40 degrees exiting over a stile into another field. Carry on ahead to exit through a gap into another field, then exiting over a stile to a lane. Here turn right passing Home Farm and Southmarsh Farm and in 450m walk up to a road (B3081). Cross over the road and on ahead along a lane opposite passing Knapp Farm and in 1.1kms (0.75 miles) and before Brickhouse Farm bear right across a field aiming for a gate at the right-hand end of a wooden fence at ST7446 3139. Go through this gate and the next one and on ahead along the track across a field exiting through a gate and into the northern end of Pen Forest.

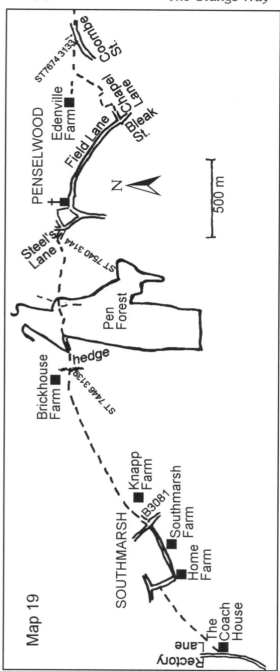

In 50m where the track swings right enter the wood ahead on an uphill track. In 300m at a cross track turn left onto Steel's Lane (track) and in 500m walk up to a lane opposite a T-junction at ST7540 3144. Here turn right and in 250m at a T-junction turn left. After 150m at a junction by St Michael's C of E church in Penselwood, turn right. After 700m along Field Lane turn left down Chapel Lane.

At its terminal point go down the footpath on the right hand side of the lane and proceed on behind residences turning left and right to go alongside a field and up to a stile. Cross over the stile and go into a field at Edenville Farm crossing at about 30 degrees. Exit over a stile where immediately turn right and in 15m join a track and on ahead up to a lane (Coombe St). Here turn left and then along Pen Mill Hill ignoring other lanes to right or left for 1.6kms (1.0 miles). Walk along Tulse Hill to Portnell's Lane and up to the main road opposite the war memorial at Zeals.

Zeals to Mere
4.1kms (2.5 miles)
Time: 1.0 hrs

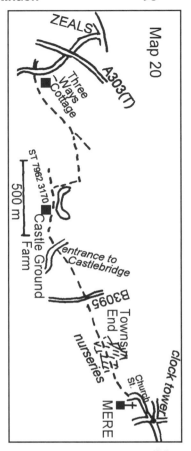

From the war memorial at Zeals walk east along the main road and in 500m at a T-junction turn right signed 'Wolverton' and go under the A303 (T). After 250m at Three Ways Cottage (**Map 20**) just before a T-junction turn left between hedgerows and go over a stile to enter a field. Continue along the right hand edge and on into another field (*or you can walk along a parallel track at this point*).

At the first junction of paths by farm buildings, turn right along a farm track on bearing about 160 degrees. Follow the track ahead and round to the left and right and to a T-junction of tracks at ST7962 3170. Here turn left continuing on past residences at Castle Ground Farm and up to the entrance of Castlebridge. Cross over the entrance track and go through a gate into a field. Cross the field on a bearing of about 60 degrees to exit over a stile to a road (B3095).

Cross over the road and go over a stile and into a field and exiting through the gate ahead and into another field exiting

The Clock Tower at Mere

Photo: L Ham

over a stile and into a nursery area at Town's End. Walk between the greenhouses exiting through a gate and into a field. Keeping to the left of the field exit through a gate and onto a road and up to a T-junction opposite the church of St Michael the Archangel at Mere. Here turn left and follow the lane round into Church St and up to the clock tower in Mere.

Mere to Hindon
10.9kms (6.75 miles) Time: 2.75 hrs

From the clock tower in Mere walk east along Salisbury Street, then turn right down Boar St. Immediately past Mere United Reformed Church turn left along Dark Lane. At the end of Dark Lane turn right and after 200m turn left down a metalled lane to go over a footbridge and up to another lane. Here turn left, and in 40m, just beyond a telegraph pole turn right along the footpath between hedgerows signposted to 'Charnage'. Exit to a field and continue on ahead.

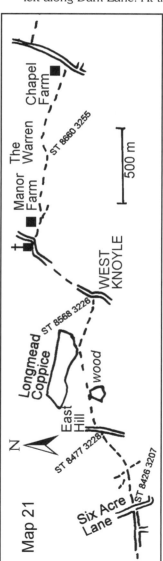

Go through a gate and across another field and on ahead through another gate and into another field. Exiting through a gate continue on ahead. Exit through a gate and into another field. Exit through a gate to a lane. Cross the lane and continue on ahead through a gate onto a track. Go through a gate and into a field continuing along the left-hand edge. Go through a gate into a field walking half-right to the southwest corner of Chaddenwick Wood. Turn left along the edge of the wood and go through a gate into a field, cross the field exiting through a gate to a lane at a T-junction.

Go forward on the lane opposite signposted to 'West Knoyle' (**Map 21**) and after walking 850m arrive at a T-junction at Six Acre Lane. Cross over the lane and over a stile and into a field. Keeping to the right-hand side cross over several stiles to exit the field in the bottom right-hand corner over a stile and ditch to a field. Here take the left footpath on bearing about 40 degrees, cross over a stile and on ahead to exit the field over a stile and through a hedgerow to a lane at ST8477 3228.

Cross over the lane and go over a stile and through a gate to cross a field aiming to the left of the wood ahead at about 80 degrees. Exit over a stile into a field. Keep to the right hand edge by the wood exiting through a gate and on ahead across a field, exiting through a gate into another field. Walk half-left across the field towards Longmead Coppice on the left and go over a stile into another field.

Cross the field on bearing about 110 degrees exiting over a stile and into another field exiting through a gate into another field and through a gate to a lane at West Knoyle at ST8568 3226. Here turn left along the lane for 600m to Manor Farm. At Manor Farm turn right and go through the farmyard taking the left-hand path up the hill, go through a gate and continue uphill always aiming for the left-hand path to the ridge. After 550m at ST8660 3255 go through a gate into a field keeping to the left-hand edge descending to exit onto a track and down to a lane by Chapel Farm.

Here turn left along the lane and in 300m turn right along a track. Maintain the main track and in 1.2kms (0.75 miles) walk up to the A350. Cross the A350 and continue on ahead for 1.4kms (0.75 miles) to a T-junction of tracks at ST8996 3260, here turn left and in 300m down towards a road (B3089). Just before the road turn right onto a well-used grassy track, which gradually diverges from the road. After 500m the track joins a minor road. Here, turn left for 50m and then right along a bridle path and subsequent surfaced road (The Dene) to emerge in Hindon at the lower end of the High St. (The village is to your left up the High St).

The route: Westbound

Hindon to Mere
10.9kms (6.75 miles) Time: 2.75 hrs

From the lower end of the High St, Hindon walk westbound along The Dene and subsequent bridle path. At a minor road turn left and then right after 50m onto a well-used grassy track for 500m. Where the track almost meets the B3089 turn left along another track and up to a cross track in 300m at ST8996 3260. Here turn right and in 1.4kms (0.75 miles) walk up to a road A350. Cross over the road and on ahead for 1.3kms (0.75 miles) to a lane, here turn left and in 300m turn right before Chapel Farm up a bridle path (**Map 21**). Then enter a field where follow the right-hand edge to the very top. Exit through the right hand of two gates to follow a path on a ridge. Descend down the ridge exiting through a gate and through Manor Farm farmyard to a lane where turn left.

Walk along the lane for 600m towards West Knoyle passing a T-junction on the right. 100m beyond a telephone box at ST8568 3226 turn right through a gate into a field. Cross the field and go through another gate into a field, go over a stile into another field. Exit in the top right hand corner into another field by Longmead Coppice on the right. Cross the field on bearing about 260 degrees to exit through a gate into another field. Go through a gate into another field, keeping to the left-hand edge by a wood. In the left-hand corner cross a stile and go across the field in the same direction, exiting through a gate to the right of a galvanised water trough and then over a stile to a lane at ST8477 3228.

Cross over the lane and go through a hedgerow and cross a stile into a field. Cross the field half-left at about 230 degrees to exit over a stile into an enclosure. Maintain direction to exit across a ditch and over a stile into a field. Keep to the left-hand edge crossing several stiles to the top left-hand corner exiting to a lane (Six Acre Lane) at a T-junction at ST8426 3207. Proceed along the lane ahead to Charnage and in 850m walk up to a T-junction.

Cross the lane and go through a gate into a field exiting in the left-hand corner through a gate then ahead alongside the southern edge of Chaddenwick Wood. Exit to a field crossing it half-right at about 320 degrees. At the corner of hedgerows across the field turn left through a gate into a field. Continue along the right hand edge of the field exiting through a gate to a track, then through a gate and up to a lane. Cross the lane and go through a gate into a field, exiting through a gate into another field. Continue in the same direction exiting through a gate into another field.

Proceed on ahead exiting through a gate into another field. Exit through double gates into another field, exiting through a gate into another field. At residences go down an enclosed path to a lane where turn left. In 40m turn right along a path and go over a footbridge before bearing slightly right and up to a T-junction. Here turn right along The Lynch, in 200m turn left along Dark Lane and into Boar St and up to Salisbury St. Here turn left to the clock tower at Mere.

Mere to Zeals
4.1kms (2.5 miles) Time: 1.0 hrs

From the clock tower in Mere (**Map 20**) walk along Church St and follow the road round the back of the church, St Michael the Archangel at Mere. Just past the Old Rectory turn right and go through a gate into a field. Exit in the right hand corner to go through a nursery area passing between greenhouses at Town's End. Exit over a stile to a field and through a gate into another field and on ahead, exiting over a stile to a road (B3095). Cross the road and go over a stile into a field crossing on a bearing of about 245 degrees exiting at the top right hand corner through a gate by the entrance to Castlebridge.

Passing the entrance to Castlebridge walk along a track opposite to Castle Ground Farm passing residences and up into a wooded area. At a T-junction of tracks turn right and in 30m take the left fork. Follow the track round left and then right to a cross track at farm buildings. Cross the track and turn left into a field keeping to the left and on into another field over two stiles. Exit over a stile in the left-hand corner and continue on between hedgerows by a residence (Three Ways cottage) and up to a lane. Here turn right along the lane passing under the A303 (T) and up to a T-junction. Here turn left and in 450m arrive at the war memorial at Zeals.

Zeals to Wincanton
9.3kms (5.75 miles) Time: 2.5 hrs

From the war memorial at Zeals cross over the road to Portnell's Lane and turn immediately left along Tulse Hill just after the Zeals exit boundary sign take the right fork into Pen Mill Hill ignoring other lanes to left or right. After 900m take the right-hand footpath through a gate at ST7674 3133 on Coombe St (Map 19) signposted to 'Edenville Farm'. Initially on a surfaced lane and in 50m bearing left onto a track behind a residence with a wood on your right. At its terminal point go to the left of a gate and in 15m go over a stile on the left and into a field crossing on bearing about 210 degrees exiting in the left hand corner over a stile.

Continue alongside a fence following the enclosed footpath left and then right exiting to Chapel Lane (cul-de-sac) and on up to a T-junction. Here turn right along Bleak St and Field Lane and in 700m up to a T-junction at Penselwood (village church of St Michael C of E on the right). Here turn left downhill signed 'Wincanton' and in 120m at a T-junction turn right, signed 'Stourton'. In 200m opposite a T-junction turn left down a track, Steel's Lane at ST7540 3144, and in 500m turn right into woodland (Pen Forest) on a track just beyond a path signposted 'Southmarsh'. After 250m join a farm track and on ahead to exit the wood in 100m through a gate into a field. Follow the track ahead exiting through two gates into another field to cross in front of Brickhouse Farm veering left to join a farm track. Here turn left and in 1.1kms (0.75 miles) after passing by Knapp Farm arrive at the B3081.

Cross over the road and walk along the lane ahead passing Southmarsh Farm and Home Farm. 120m after a right hand bend go over a stile on the left and into a field. Cross the field exiting through a gap into another field. Exit over a stile into another field to cross at about 220 degrees exiting over a stile to a lane (Rectory Lane) by The Coach House. Here turn left along the lane and in 600m just after crossing a stone bridge go left over a stile at ST7225 2992 and into a field, signposted 'Love Lane and Bayford'. Cross the field at about 225 degrees exiting over a stile and into another field and on ahead. Go over a stile and into another field and on ahead. Exit over a stile and into another field and on ahead.

Exit over a double stile and into another field and on ahead. Exit over a footbridge to another field. Keeping to the right exit over a stile to cross a track and on ahead. In 50m cross over a stile and up into a field continuing along the right hand edge to cross over a stile and into the neck of a field to follow the hedgerow round to the right. Exit on the right hand edge of the field in the corner behind residences. Go over a stile and on ahead to join a lane by Windmill Farmhouse. Walk along the lane (Grants Lane, then Ireson Lane) and down to the High St in Wincanton.

Section 8

Hindon to Salisbury

Map: OS Explorer 143, 130
Start: High St/The Dene crossroads Hindon
Finish: Salisbury Cathedral
Distance: 29.7kms (18.25 miles)
Time: 7.75hrs
Transport: Railway: Salisbury
                 Buses: Hindon, Berwick St Leonard, Fonthill Bishop,
Teffont, Dinton, Quidhampton, and Salisbury (Wilton and Bemerton
infrequently)
Place of historical interest: Berwick St Leonard, Wilton House, Salisbury
Cathedral, and Bishop's Palace Salisbury

The history

The Prince left Wincanton and breakfasted at Berwick St Leonard, travelling on through Teffont, Dinton, Wylye and Wilton on the way to Salisbury. Prince William went to see Wilton House and gardens, the seat of Thomas Herbert, the eighth Earl of Pembroke. It was at Wilton House that William was joined by the Prince of Denmark.

William entered the city of Salisbury at about 3 o' clock in the afternoon as recorded by the Revd Whittle:

'The manner of their Entrance into this City, was far more glorious than that of Exeter: for here the Mayor and Aldermen met his Highness the Prince of Orange in all their Formalities. First of all marched the Regiment of Foot Guards belonging to Count Solms, with their Colours flying, Drums beating, Hoitboys playing: the People thronging in the Street, and making great Acclamations. Next, some Troops of Horse, with their Kettle-Drums beating, Trumpets sounding, the officers shewing their Courtesy to the People: Then came his highness the Prince of Orange, with the Prince of Denmark on his right Hand, and the Duke of Ormond on his Left. Never were windows more crowded with Faces of both Sexes than here: never were Bells ringing more melodiously? than now at Sarum: never were People shouting and echoing forth Huzza's in the Air more than now. The Bishop's Palace there being the best and most meet place, both the Princes rode thither, altho afterwards his Highness Prince George went to the quarters assign'd him'

Prince William was now occupying the lodgings vacated by the fleeing king, the Bishop's Palace. Quiet a lot happened in Salisbury that concerned both Prince William and King James, it was a turning point in the campaign. Salisbury had been King James' headquarters during the crisis and it was here that he held council meetings that would eventually decide the future course of action – or inaction.

The old Bishop's Palace now occupied by the Salisbury Cathedral School was the King's lodgings. It was here that the second blood of the bloodless revolution was spilled – King James'. King James had intended to confront Prince William on Salisbury Plain but events unfolded to cause a radical change to his plans. William's plan had always been to disintegrate James's army by means of defections that had been arranged. James began to find his army deserting him, some officers advised him to retreat to London. John Churchill his most able commander fled to join Prince William others followed. These desertions had a great effect on King James who suffered a psychosomatic nosebleed of the first order, which could not be staunched for several days. Orders were given to retreat – a turning point in more ways than one.

Indeed James must have felt very betrayed as recalled later by Victorian historian T B Macaulay:

'Before he [James] set out for Salisbury, he called together the officers who were in London and made them the following speech'

'according to the lords partition. I have engaged my royal word to call a free parliament as soon as ever the prince of Orange has quitted these kingdoms; and I am resolved to do everything which is in my power to quiet the minds of my people, by securing their religion, laws and liberty; if you desire anything more I am ready to grant it; but after all this, if any of you are not satisfied, let him declare himself; I am willing to grant passes to all such as are willing to go over to the prince of Orange and spare them the shame of deserting their lawful sovereign'. 'Among the officers addressed were the duke of Grafton, lord Churchill and Cols Kirk and Trelawney, who with the rest of the assembly, assured the King that they were satisfied and that they were ready to spill the last drop of blood in his service'.

The route: Eastbound

Hindon to Dinton
12.2kms (8.0 miles) Time: 3.25 hrs

From the crossroads at High St and The Dene (**Map 22**)at the lower end of High St walk in an easterly direction along The Dene, forking right to join a track where turn left. Proceed for 500m to a road (B3089) where turn right. Walk along the road for about 700m to Berwick St Leonard turning left down the second access road signposted 'Berwick Courtyard Fonthill Estates'. (*The first turning is a private road*). Follow the road round to the left past a car park to turn right over a bridge and up to a T-junction.

At this point should you wish to visit the church at Berwick St Leonard, turn left and follow the track to its terminal point and fork right to enter the churchyard – returning the same way.

Here turn right along a lane by cottages. At the end of the lane go through a gate and cross a field exiting over a stile into another field. Exit over a stile into another field exiting through a gate into the graveyard of All Saints C of E

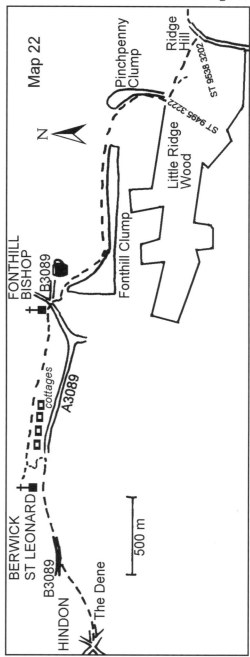

Map 22

N

FONTHILL BISHOP

B3089

Pinchpenny Clump

Ridge Hill

ST 9538 3202

ST 9495 3222

Little Ridge Wood

Fonthill Clump

A3089

cottages

BERWICK ST LEONARD

B3089

HINDON

The Dene

500 m

church at Fonthill Bishop. Continue on passing to the right of the church and exiting to the B3089.

Cross the road and go behind the bus shelter to turn right and past the gable end of a building. Turn left before the first gate and pass through a courtyard area and onto a concrete track leading uphill. Follow the track round the edge of a wood (Fonthill Clump) on the right and on ahead to pass Pinchpenny Clump on the left.

Follow the path down across a valley floor and through a narrow band of trees and up into Little Ridge Wood soon going left at ST9495 3222. At a Y-junction take the left fork and up to a wider track where turn left and on to a gate and a lane at ST9538 3202. Here turn left and in 10m take the right-hand fork road. Continue past a T-junction on the right and an offset crossroads and on ahead on bearing about 100 degrees with a wood on the right. After 1.4kms (0.75 miles) go straight across offset crossroads and down a short lane for 50m to further crossroads. Continue on downhill and after 200m turn right by cottages at ST9717 3205. (**Map 23**)

Go though a gate and on ahead alongside Cleeve Copse for 950m leaving and re-entering the copse along the route. At ST9805 3175 turn right outside the western edge of a wood and left in 200m on to a track. Follow this track later surfaced for 1.1kms (0.75 miles) and up to a T-junction. Here turn left and in 60m carry on up to a T-junction with the B3089. Turn left and in 300m, opposite Pear Tree Cottage, turn right up a footpath by a residence up into a wooded area.

When the track levels out at a cross track turn right and go downhill between fences exiting through a gate.

Continue between fences across a field through a gate and then a wood. Exit from the wood and continue across offset cross paths along a track. Follow the track round and alongside a wood and go through a gate into Dinton Park. In 50m cross over a stile and into a field. Cross the field below Philipps House aiming for the church at Dinton. Then bearing slightly right exiting through a gate into a car park at SU0100 3162. Go through the National Trust car park to the road and turn left and proceed up to St Mary's church Dinton.

Dinton to Salisbury
17.5kms (10.75 miles)
Time: 4.5 hrs

From St Mary's Church Dinton walk north past Dinton Lodge opposite and turn immediately right up an enclosed footpath. Go through a gate and across a field on bearing about 75 degrees to exit through a gate into another field. Keeping to the right-hand side of the field exit through a gate to a track. Continue on ahead and at a junction of paths go straight ahead to enter a field through a gate.

Proceed on ahead exiting in the right-hand corner between residences and up to a road (Spracklands). Bear slightly left and go between residences on a footpath to then enter a field through a gate. Cross the field exiting through a gate to pass to the left of East Farm buildings and up to a lane. Cross over the lane and enter Manor Farm. Go through the farmyard turning left, then right through a gate and into a field. Cross the field and go over a stile and on ahead, then over a stile into another field. Carry on ahead along the edge of the field with a wooded area on the left.

In the top left-hand corner go over a stile and into the wood. Go up through the wood and 15m before the field turn right on bearing about 60 degrees. Still in the wood keep to left hand paths parallel to the field descending to a track. Here turn right for 50m and up to farm buildings at a *second* Manor Farm. Turn left on a track to a lane at SU0288 3227. Here turn left

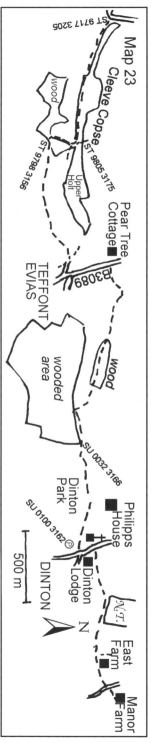

along the lane. In 600m where the lane turns left go right up a track and in a further 600m to a cross track at SU0357 3318.

Here turn right along the Ox Drove track for 2.3kms (1.5 miles) and just after where the track becomes a surfaced lane at SU0571 3242 continue eastwards up a broad track keeping to the Ox Drove track. At a cross track in 2.1kms (1.25 miles) continue on ahead for 700m to a T-junction of tracks at Ugford Red Buildings, here turn right down a double width track ideally taking the left-hand track downhill. At a Y-junction in 700m take the left-hand fork to pass behind residences and down to a road where turn right under a railway arch and up to the A30.

Here turn left and into Wilton along West St. Cross over a junction with traffic lights and into Silver St and then past Wilton House and up to a roundabout. Here turn right along the A36 (T) and in 600m at traffic lights turn right onto the A3094 down Netherhampton Rd.

In 300m at a T-junction turn left into Quidhampton and in 700m at a Y-junction bear right to Bemerton. After 1km at Church Lane go to the right of a small flint church along a lane into Lower Bemerton and in 400m turn right along a footpath marked 'West Harnham'.

Follow the winding path and eventually after crossing a footbridge fork to the left at a junction of paths. Then on to arrive at a road junction on a bend at Upper St and Middle St. Here turn left into Middle St and at its end where it joins Lower St turn left down to the Old Mill, crossing weirs and sluices over the River Avon. Cross over the Long Bridge passing Harnham Water Meadows on the left. Go over a footbridge and up to a road where turn right and into Mill St, then Crane Bridge Rd and Crane St. Turn right into High St and go through an arch into the Cathedral grounds and proceed up to Salisbury Cathedral.

The route: Westbound

Salisbury to Dinton
17.5kms (10.75 miles) Time: 4.5 hrs

From Salisbury Cathedral west door walk north through an arch to High St. Left into Crane St and continue over the bridge over the River Avon and into Mill Rd. In 150m bear left and cross a footbridge and then the Long Bridge over the River Avon passing Harnham Water Meadows on the right. Then re-cross the river at the Old Mill and up to a T-junction at Lower St and Middle St. Turn right into Middle St and continue to a sharp left-hand bend where it joins Upper St.

At this point turn right on a footpath marked 'Bemerton' alongside the River Nadder. Follow the main footpath ignoring footpaths to left or right to cross a series of footbridges and up to a road at Bemerton. Here turn left and walk through the village for 1.4kms (0.75 miles) to a Y-junction at Quidhampton, here turn left and walk through the village and up to a T-junction (A3094) in 700m.

Here turn right and in 300m up to the A36 (T) where turn left. In 600m at a roundabout turn left along the A30 into Wilton crossing the River Wylye and passing Wilton House on the left. Follow the A30 round into Silver St and across a junction with traffic lights into West St and on ahead. Just after where

the A30 turns left turn right along a road called Water Ditchampton, road signs to 'Great Wishford', and in 200m pass under a railway arch. Here immediately turn half-left up a track going past cottages and uphill to join a path coming in from the left in a wooded area.

Continuing uphill on a broad double track between trees. At a point where the track ahead splits into two distinct tracks beyond Ugford Red Buildings at SU0840 3235 turn left onto Ox Drove track at about 290 degrees between trees. At a cross track in 700m continue on ahead and up to a junction with a road after a further 2.1kms (1.25 miles). Here turn right along the road (*signpost reads 'road used as public path'*) and at a Y-junction after 400m

Salisbury Cathedral

Photo: L Ham

continue on the main left-hand track. In 700m cross a track and on ahead and in a further 1.3kms (0.75 miles) arrive at a cross track with the Monarch's Way coming in from the right at SU0357 3318.

Here turn left down a track and in 600m to join a lane and in a further 600m turn right up a track by Manor Farm. After 50m by farm buildings turn right on a track for another 50m and then left into a wood before a field (*path not signposted*). Follow this path which runs close to the right-hand edge of the wood. At a point where the faint track turns downhill follow it down to cross a stile into a field at SU0255 3216. Here turn right and continue along the right-hand edge of the field. In the right hand corner cross over a stile and into another field continuing on ahead exiting over a stile into a field and on ahead to enter the <u>second</u> Manor Farm buildings through a gate (**Map 23**). Go to the left through the farmyard exiting to a lane.

Cross over the lane and passing to the right of East Farm buildings and through a gate into a field and on ahead exiting through a gate to a footpath by residences. Follow the path round to a road (Spracklands) and cross slightly left to go between residences and through a gate to a field and on ahead and then through another gate and on ahead. At a T-junction of paths continue on ahead, where the path turns right go through a gate and on ahead across a field keeping to the left-hand side. In the bottom left hand corner exit through a gate to cross a field on bearing about 260 degrees, or aiming for the church. Exit by a stone and brick building through a gate and onto an enclosed path, exiting at a road opposite St Mary's church Dinton.

Dinton to Hindon
12.2kms (8.0 miles) Time: 3.25 hrs

From St Mary's church Dinton walk south down the lane to the National Trust car park on the right. Go through the car park and a wooded area and enter Dinton Park over a stile into a field. Cross the field bearing west, keeping below Philipps House. Then aiming for the right-hand edge of a wood to exit over a stile at SU0032 3166 and in 40m through a gate leaving Dinton Park. Follow this track alongside a wood for 200m then bearing right for a further 300m to another wood. Here turn right and in 5m turn left to go through the centre of the wood exiting after 300m. Cross a track and go through a gate and in 200m enter a wood through a gate. Follow the path ahead and in 200m, before a gate, bear left downhill and between hedgerows exiting at a road (B3089) opposite Pear Tree Cottage.

Here turn left along the road for 300m to a T-junction on a bend. Here turn right on a lane to Teffont Evias. In 60m turn right along a lane and track for 1.1kms (0.75 miles), then turn right at ST9798 3156 on a path outside the western edge of a wood for 200m. At a T-junction of paths at ST9805 3175 turn left and on ahead into Cleeve Copse maintaining the same direction for 950m leaving and re-entering the copse along the route exiting through a gate and down to a lane on a bend by cottages at ST9717 3205.

Here turn left and in 200m at a crossroads cross over and in a further 50m, at an offset crossroads continue on ahead on a lane signposted to 'Ridge'. After 1.4kms (0.75 miles) at an offset crossroads carry on for a further 200m past a left turn. Just past where a road joins from the right turn right through a gate at ST9538 3202 (**Map 22**) and proceed along a track.

After 200m at a Y-junction take a narrow footpath leading off to the right to join a wider track. At a Y-junction take the right hand fork down through trees to arrive at a point where the track swings right at ST9495 3222. Follow the track round to the right leaving Little Ridge Wood to cross a valley floor between a narrow band of trees. Then on past Pinchpenny Clump on the right and later Fonthill Clump on the left. Exit through a courtyard and turning right to a road opposite Fonthill Bishop All Saints C of E church.

Cross the road and enter the church grounds passing to the left of the church and into a second graveyard. Exit through a gate into a field. Cross the field and exit over a stile into another field and over another stile into another field. Exit through a gate onto a lane soon passing cottages on your left at Berwick St Leonard and after 200m up to a T-junction.

At this point should you wish to visit the church at Berwick St Leonard, carry on this track to its terminal point and fork right to enter the churchyard – returning the same way, as the exit road to the west of the church is a private road.

Here turn left over a bridge and left again past a car park and up to a road, the B3089 where turn right. In 700m bear left along a track and in 500m bear right down a track to exit from The Dene at the lower end of High St Hindon. *The village is to your right up the High St.*

Salisbury to Collingbourne Kingston

Map: OS Explorer 130, 131
Start: Salisbury Cathedral
Finish: St Mary C of E Church in Collingbourne Kingston
Distance: 44.6kms (27.75 miles)
Time: 11.5 hrs
Transport: Railway: Salisbury
                Buses: Salisbury, Gt Durnford (infrequent), Amesbury,
Larkhill, (Bulford, Netheravon, hourly from Salisbury), (Everleigh, infrequently),
(Collingbourne Kingston, hourly from Andover)
Place of historical interest: Salisbury Cathedral, Bishop's Palace Salisbury,
Old Sarum and Stonehenge (visited by William's army)

Special Note: On this section it is necessary to cross a military area at Larkhill Artillery Ranges after Amesbury, which is frequently closed to the public. Please phone 01980 620819 or 07810 674763 (answering machine with range closure details) to check before setting out. In the event of the ranges being closed an alternative route is suggested going from Amesbury to Netheravon via Bulford – see page 113.

The history

Prince William rested for one night at Salisbury and left to march to Amesbury, some of his army took a 'Cook's Tour' at this point visiting Stonehenge to witness one of the 'Wonders of the World'. Whittle describes the scene as they left Salisbury:

'After some stay here, the Prince of Orange went to Ambury, attended with the Duke of Ormond, and many of the English Nobility and Gentry, besides Dutch, Scotch and French. The first Line was advanced towards the most renowned City of London, a considerable way, the roads here being good for marching: and as the regiments marched over the Plains, they made pleasant Figures, sometimes marching in Battalia, and sometimes marching in a Line: The Weather now was favourable, and the way very good. And being to march near one of the Wonders of the World, called Stonehenge, most Regiments made a halt to view this strange Sight: none that saw it could render any satisfactory Account concerning it: Certain Officers ask'd the minister of Ambury what was his Opinion, because they presumed 'twas within the Bounds of his Parish: who told them, that he supposed it to be a Trophy, or Monument erected in token of some notable Victory which was obtain'd there: I must confess, this is the general Opinion of the greatest Antiquaries of our Nation.' 'The Custom of erecting a Trophy, or Monument, in token of Victory is

*of great Antiquity, and first began among the Greeks, who used in
that place where the enemies were vanquish'd to cut down the Boughs
of great Trees, and in the Stocks, or Bodies of them, to hang up
Armour, or other Spoils, taken from the Enemy. Others argued
strongly that these prodigious Stones were brought out of Ireland by
Merlin's Magical Art, and curiously fram'd and put together. To
corroborate this Opinion, they assured us, that a piece broken off
from these Stones, and put into the Wall of any Well, or cast into the
Water, shall, for certain, kill and destroy all venemous Creatures
therin.'*

At Amesbury the Revd Whittle records:

*'To proceed the Army moved daily according to the Motion of his
Highness, who rode from Ambury unto a certain Gentleman's House
near Collingburn'*

On this section the open plains of Wiltshire now lie ahead.

The Weary Walker

*A plain in front of me,
And there's the road
Upon it. Wide country,
And, too, the road!*

*Past the first ridge another
And still the road
Creeps on. Perhaps no other
Ridge for the road?*

*Ah! Past a third ridge,
Which still the road
Has to climb furtherward –
The thin white road!*

*Sky seems to end its track;
But no. The road
Trails down the hill at the back.
Ever the road!*

Thomas Hardy

The route: Eastbound

Salisbury to Amesbury
16.3kms (10.0 miles) Time: 4.0 hrs

From the west entrance at Salisbury Cathedral walk north through an arch to High St. Turn left into Crane St and in 100m turn right by a bridge to follow the River Avon and up to Bridge St where turn right. In 20m turn left across the road to cross over the River Avon by a footbridge. Then go through an archway to regain the riverside and on ahead. Maintain this riverside path passing by a coach park before reaching Mill Stream Approach. Crossing roads and continuing ahead go under two bridges and several roads.

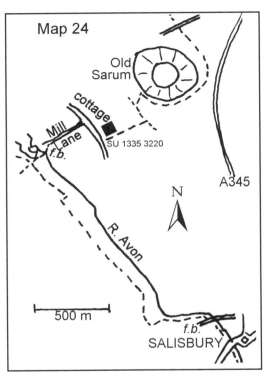

Eventually cross a footbridge (**Map 24**) over a small stream and then on along a raised earth bank to join a raised wooden path. At a gate turn left staying on the raised wooden path. Turn right on reaching a gravel path after 80m. Follow this path for 900m to cross a tarmac path where turn right to cross the River Avon by a footbridge. The path becomes a lane (Mill Lane) and up to a road where turn right. In 200m turn left at a thatched and flintstone walled cottage at SU1335 3220 on a track towards Old Sarum. After 400m at a junction of paths by a gate turn left before it, and at a Y-junction turn right uphill to the outer ramparts of Old Sarum. Carry straight on and walk round the southern side to the east side of Old Sarum exiting through a gate to the main entrance road. Here turn right and in 50m turn left and immediately right through two gates to follow a path between fences outside Old Sarum grounds to arrive at a road.

Cross over the road and follow the track ahead. After passing Shepherds Corner in 600m maintain same direction up and over a low ridge to pass Keepers Cottage in a further 1.2kms (0.75 miles). Continue on the track ahead, uphill and in 800m follow a footpath into a small wood to exit through a gate into a field. Carry on ahead with a fence on the left to cross a track in 500m and in a further 700m up to a gate at a concrete road at SU1352 3645, here turn left. Follow a concrete road for 700m up to a lane where turn right and in 150m turn left along the lane to Great Durnford (**Map 25**). After 1.2kms (0.75 miles) downhill and through the village go up to a T-junction where turn right and walk along the winding lane for 800m, passing the entrance to Great Durnford Manor, to turn left at SU1409 3857, uphill on a track on the edge of Ham Wood. On leaving the wood after 500m bear right onto a footpath through a small wooded area exiting at a gate and into a field, here turn right at SU1390 3920.

Maintain direction across fields for 700m, with fence on right-hand side and crossing one track to arrive at a gate and walk on into a hilly field. Continue ahead following a feint track before finally veering slightly right to exit through a gate and on to a track at the far

Map 25

GREAT
DURNFORD

SU 139 391

500 m

SU 1409 3857

Ham Wood

To Stonehenge

Church Street

Salisbury Street

Alternative Route to Netheravon

f.b.

R. Avon

farm track

N

end and at the bottom of a slope. Follow the track crossing a farm track after 500m and in a further 400m to a junction of paths. Go straight on ahead crossing the River Avon by a series of footbridges and up to a junction by a car park. Here turn left exiting Recreation Rd to a road on a bend at the junction of Stonehenge Rd and Church St. (*Walkers going onto Stonehenge turn left into Stonehenge Rd and pick up the route direction on the second line of the Amesbury to Netheravon via Stonehenge section. For Amesbury continue with this description*). Go forward along Church St to re-cross the River Avon and up to a T-junction with High St and Salisbury St in Amesbury.

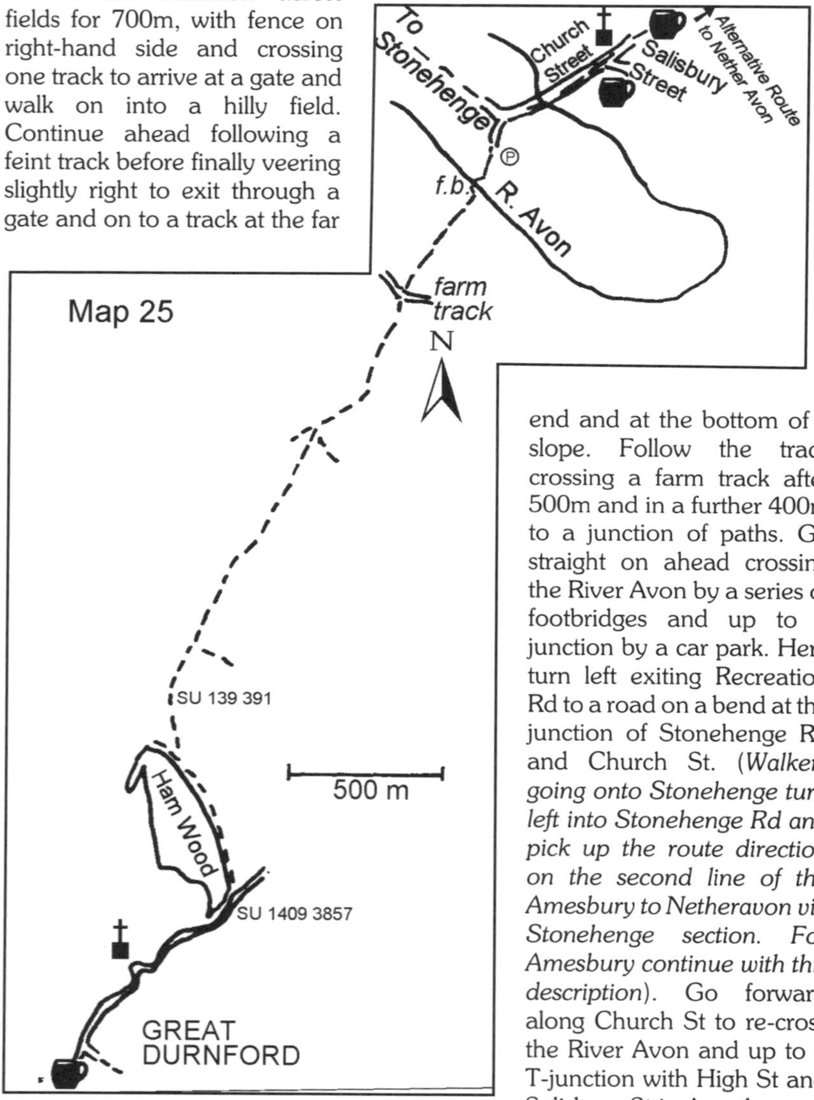

Amesbury to Netheravon via Stonehenge
13.5kms (8.5 miles) Time: 3.5 hrs

Special Note: On this leg it is necessary to cross a military area at Larkhill Artillery Ranges, which is frequently closed to the public. The flying of red flags on the entry points to the ranges indicates range closures. Please phone 01980 620819 or 07810 674763 (answering machine with range closure details) to check before setting out. In the event of the ranges being closed an alternative route is suggested going from Amesbury to Netheravon via Bulford, see page 113.

From the T-junction of Church St, High St and Salisbury St in Amesbury walk west along Church St, crossing the River Avon and at the end of Church St bear right into Stonehenge Rd. Follow the footpath alongside Stonehenge Rd for 1.6kms (1.0 miles) to join the A303 (T). Continue to walk westbound on the footpath alongside the road and at the crest of a hill catching sight of Stonehenge directly ahead. At Stonehenge Bottom where the footpath ends at a Y-junction with the A344, cross over the A303 (T) (*taking great care*) and also cross the A344 to join a footpath on the right-hand side of the A344. Turn left and walk up the hill to Stonehenge.

Enter a car park on the right and then turning left walk to the far end of the car park exiting in the right-hand corner through a gate to a track. Here turn right and in 700m in a dip cross 'The Cursus' (*Once thought to be a Roman racecourse but archeological evidence dates it to 3000BC*). Continuing on the track ahead and after passing the entrance to Durrington Down Farm walk up to a road at a bend, Fargo Rd coming in from the right and Willoughby Rd on ahead. Go forward up Willoughby Rd to its terminal point in 600m at a T-junction, with an ambulance station on the right. Here turn left along The Packway to walk on the grass verge alongside it. After 800m, at the end of the

Stonehenge

tree line on the left, turn right up a broad track at SU1175 4445 (**Map 26**).

You are now entering a military area. Walking round the military establishment at Larkhill first passing by the fenced military area at Knighton Down, continue on the broad track round to the right. After 1.2kms (0.75 miles) where a track comes in from the left at SU1249 4500 follow the track round to the left alongside Cutt's Copse, on the right. At the end of the copse the track joins another from the left, here bear right and follow the line of a boundary fence with buildings on the other side. Then soon passing a sports field on the right and up to a junction of tracks at the corner of the sports field at SU1285 4541.

Continue forward northwards down to a nearby horse racetrack area bearing right to negotiate a route passing between the course officials buildings and then descending to the fence surrounding the horse racetrack. Here turn right alongside the racetrack and follow it round to the left gradually heading northbound. Go over a crosstrack and continue along the racetracks eastern edge on bearing about 340 degrees for almost 600m to a Y-junction at SU1320 4648. Here bear right along a grassy track and in 300m ignoring crosstracks go diagonally through a wide gap in Anniversary Plantation.

Exit the plantation and ignoring crosstracks maintain the main track ahead for 900m to a crosstrack junction area. Maintain direction on the track opposite soon passing a military flagpole at a Y-junction at SU1343 4779. Bear right ahead on a track, which soon becomes surfaced. After a further 300m **pass out of the military area** and go down to a junction with a lane at SU1387 4840. Here turn right and in 700m up to a T-junction with the A345. Here turn left and in 25m turn right and in 200m up to a T-junction at a small triangular green in Netheravon.

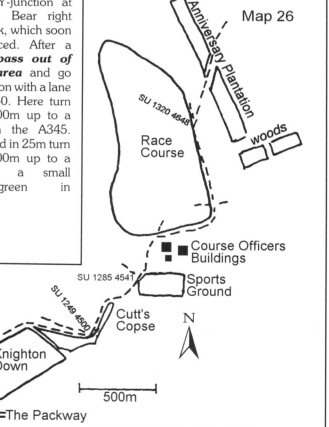

Map 26

Alternative route from Amesbury to Netheravon if Larkhill Artillery Ranges are closed to the public.

Amesbury to Netheravon via Bulford
9.0kms (5.5 miles) Time: 2.25 hrs

From the T-junction of Church St, High St and Salisbury St in Amesbury walk east along High St. Cross over the A345 at traffic lights and walk up London Rd. After 450m turn left along Ratfyn Rd and after 200m go left on a footpath leading downhill through trees to cross over the A303 (T) on a footbridge and up to a road where turn left. After 250m at a junction turn right and in 40m at a Y-junction take the left-hand track across a field at about 10 degrees. Soon after passing under electricity transmission lines, follow for a short distance, a parallel footpath on the right-hand side. Soon afterwards bear right off the track onto a footpath down to a gate continuing down by a wood to a concrete lane where turn right and up to a lane on a bend.

Here turn left and in 50m before 'The Dovecote' turn right over a stile into a field keeping to the left-hand edge. Go through a gap into another field and exiting in the left-hand corner over a stile and footbridge to cross a green to a gate at a road at Bulford. Cross over the road (A3028) and go ahead up Church Lane by St Leonard's church. Go past Manor Farm and where the surfaced lane turns left into a bungalow continue ahead into a field keeping to the left-hand edge.

After 500m go left over a stile through the hedgerow line and continue on ahead on the right-hand side of the field. Go through fields, over a stile, and aim for the wooded area to the left of the Upper Farm buildings ahead. Cross a stile and enter the wooded area. Follow the footpath and exit into a lane by Mill Cottage and turn left. At the end of the lane turn left along a tarmac footpath, which swings right and crosses the River Avon, in 150m turn right again and re-cross the river going forward to a lane. Turn right and in 150m turn left onto a footpath by the side of a house and into a field. go forward in the same direction crossing three fields then aim for the right-hand side of the wooded area ahead.

Then arriving at a lane where turn right and in 30m turn left by a telephone box going between residences. After 40m enter a grassy area and proceed ahead on bearing about 355 degrees crossing a military road and reaching a line of trees. Cross a track and enter a wooded area and in a further 600m after having crossed a farm lane up to a farm track. Here turn left and exit to a road where turn right. After 50m opposite Ablington Farm turn left up a path by a large thatched house. Then on ahead passing the end of a cul-de-sac and once clear of residences carry on the same direction. Cross two fields and on through the car park of Figheldean Recreation Ground and up to a road.

Cross over the road and on ahead on an enclosed path between residences. At a Y-junction of paths follow the right hand path by smallholdings. Follow the path round to the right, when the path and tree line turns sharply right, take a left-hand footpath into the tree line exiting down to a road where turn left down to a Y-junction of lanes at SU1554 4785. Maintain the same direction towards Upavon and in 200m turn left over a stile and into a field. Follow the left-hand fence and on reaching the sewage works cross a stile and follow the right-hand fence. When it turns right take a line across a field on bearing about 320 degrees aiming for the left of a large bricked house. Exit to a road where turn left and in 400m walk to a T-junction at a small triangular green in Netheravon.

Netheravon to Everleigh
9.2kms (5.75 miles) Time: 2.5 hrs

From the small triangular green in Netheravon walk through the village along the High St marked to 'Fittleton'. Walk out of the village and into the next village of Haxton in 800m. At Haxton where the road swings right at the village centre turn left to Fittleton. Follow the road through Fittleton for a further 800m to a T-junction where turn left to Coombe. In 500m at a T junction at Coombe turn right up Coombe Lane (**Map 27**) and on ahead for 3.3kms (2.0 miles) ignoring all other paths to left or right and passing some large barns to arrive at the southern end of Dreweatt's Clump at SU1795 5185.

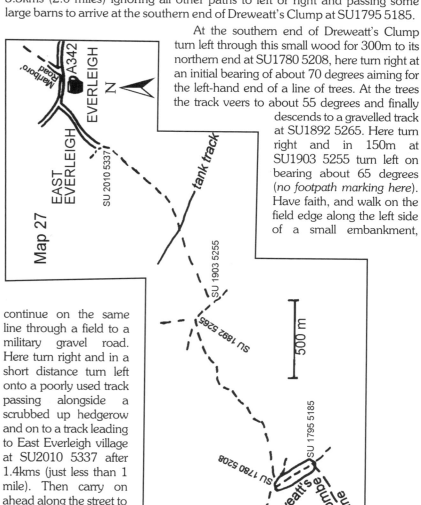

At the southern end of Dreweatt's Clump turn left through this small wood for 300m to its northern end at SU1780 5208, here turn right at an initial bearing of about 70 degrees aiming for the left-hand end of a line of trees. At the trees the track veers to about 55 degrees and finally descends to a gravelled track at SU1892 5265. Here turn right and in 150m at SU1903 5255 turn left on bearing about 65 degrees (*no footpath marking here*). Have faith, and walk on the field edge along the left side of a small embankment, continue on the same line through a field to a military gravel road. Here turn right and in a short distance turn left onto a poorly used track passing alongside a scrubbed up hedgerow and on to a track leading to East Everleigh village at SU2010 5337 after 1.4kms (just less than 1 mile). Then carry on ahead along the street to a T-junction with the A342.

Everleigh to Collingbourne Kingston
5.6kms (3.5 miles) Time: 1.5 hrs

From Everleigh village and the junction with the A342 turn right and walk along the A342 for 200m and turn left onto Marlborough Rd (signposted 'Pewsey'). Continue along Marlborough Rd for 1.7kms (1.0 miles) and turn right on a surfaced farm track to Summer Down Farm at SU2090 5524. After 100m where the surfaced track turns left, go through a gate and onto a broad track for 2.9kms (1.75 miles), which becomes Mill Drove, and on down to a road at a T-junction (A338) at SU2390 5545, here turn left into Collingbourne Kingston to arrive at St Mary C of E church after 400m.

The route: Westbound

Collingbourne Kingston to Everleigh
5.6kms (3.5 miles) Time: 1.5 hrs

From St Mary C of E church on the A338 in Collingbourne Kingston walk south along the road for 400m to a T-junction at SU2390 5545. Here turn right up a lane known as Mill Drove continuing on ahead for 2.9kms (1.75 miles) exiting through a gate to a surfaced farm track. In a 100m go forward up to a road (Marlborough Rd) where turn left. Walk along the road for 1.7kms (1.0 miles) to a T-junction (A342) (**Map 27**) where turn right and in 200m take the second left into East Everleigh village.

Everleigh to Netheravon
9.2kms (5.75 miles) Time: 2.5 hrs

From East Everleigh village walk west along the street to its terminal point at SU2010 5337, here follow the left hand track round to the right and on ahead at about 220 degrees and alongside a scrubbed up hedgerow until arriving at a military gravel road. Cross the road and continue across a field descending on bearing about 250 degrees on to arrive at a gravel track at SU1903 5255. Here turn right and in 150m at SU1892 5265 turn left up a track on bearing about 310 degrees and up a slope. Continue in this general direction to the right-hand edge of a line of trees, then veer left on bearing about 280 degrees to arrive at the northern end of Dreweatt's Clump at SU1780 5208.

Here turn left through this small wood for 300m to its southern end at SU1795 5185. Here turn right along a graveled track for 3.3kms (2.0 miles) ignoring tracks to left or right eventually becoming Coombe Lane and down to a T-junction in the village of Coombe. Here turn left and in 500m walk to a T-junction where turn right and walk through the village of Fittleton and on to Haxton after 800m. At a T-junction in Haxton turn right and in 800m up to a T-junction at a small triangular green in Netheravon.

Netheravon to Amesbury via Stonehenge
13.5kms (8.5 miles) Time: 3.5 hrs

Special Note: On this leg it is necessary to cross a military area at Larkhill Artillery Ranges, which on some occasions maybe closed to the public. The flying of red flags on the entry points to the ranges indicates range closures. Please phone 01980 620819 or 07810 674763 (answering machine with range closure details) to check before setting out. In the event of the ranges being closed an alternative route is suggested going from Netheravon to Amesbury via Bulford see page 117.

From the T-junction at a small triangular green in Netheravon walk along the road marked 'Amesbury' and 'Salisbury' and up to a T-junction with the A345. Here turn left and in 25m turn right up a lane. After 700m at a crosstrack south of Wexland Farm turn left up a lane. In 400m **enter the danger zone of Larkhill Artillery Ranges** and in a further 400m arrive at a Y-junction and a flag post at SU1343 4779. Bear left and cross over a track and carry on bearing about 190 degrees on an unsurfaced track. Maintain this track ignoring other tracks to left or right and after 900m go through a wide diagonal gap in Anniversary Plantation. (**Map 26**)

Exit to continue in the same direction for a further 300m to join a cross track by a 'point to point race course' at SU1320 4648. Here turn left and follow the edge of the racecourse, crossing a crosstrack after 600m. Continue round to the right, round the edge of the course, and once opposite the course officials' buildings, bear left to pass to the right of them, aiming for the right-hand edge of a wooded area ahead. Cross over a track and up to a fenced sports ground at SU1285 4541. Go forward on a broad track then bearing round to the right passing a fenced area of buildings.

After leaving the buildings, and in a further 100m at a Y-junction by a wooded area, turn left to walk beside Cutt's Copse on the left on bearing about 190 degrees. The track swings right at ST1249 4500. Maintain the main track alongside a wooded area bearing left round the fenced 'Knighton Down' and so down to a road at SU1175 4445 called The Packway, **leaving the military area**. Here turn left and walk along the grass verge for 800m. At a T-junction turn right down Willoughby Rd. After 600m at its terminal point where it meets Fargo Rd go forward on the lane ahead. After the passing the entrance to Durrington Down Farm the lane becomes an unsurfaced track.

On passing a copse on the right the first view of Stonehenge is gained directly ahead. On leaving the copse and in a dip cross over 'The Cursus' (*Once thought to be a Roman racecourse but archeological evidence dates it to 3000BC*). In a further 700m arrive at a car park just before the A344. Turn left through a gate to walk across to the far end of the car park exiting to the A344 at Stonehenge.

Turn left and walk along a roadside footpath for 500m to a Y-junction with the A303 (T). Cross over the A344 and then the A303 (T) (*taking great care*) turning left to walk on an uphill footpath alongside the A303 (T). On the crest of the hill is the last opportunity to look back and see Stonehenge. Proceed on then bearing right down Stonehenge Rd maintaining the same footpath. After 1.6kms (1.0 miles) arrive at a bend where turn left into Church St. (*If continuing on to Salisbury turn right at this point into Recreation Rd. For further directions refer to second line of section Amesbury to Salisbury). If walking into Amesbury* continue on along Church St. Go forward along Church St to cross the River Avon and into Amesbury to a T-junction with High St and Salisbury St.

Alternative route from Netheravon to Amesbury if Larkhill Artillery Ranges are closed to the public.

Netheravon to Amesbury via Bulford
9.0kms (5.5 miles) Time: 2.25 hrs

From the T-junction and small triangular green in Netheravon turn left along the road signposted 'Milston' to cross the River Avon before Choulston Farm. After 400m at Choulston Farm turn right over a stile into a field. Cross the field on bearing of about 140 degrees aiming for the right-hand side of the sewage works ahead. Follow the fence and cross a stile when the fence turns left, then follow the fence on the right to exit onto a road where turn right. After 200m at a Y-junction of lanes at SU1554 4785 carry on a ahead for a further 50m and find a footpath through a line of trees to a path between fields and trees, follow the path right keeping parallel to the lane to Figheldean then pass by smallholdings. Follow the path round to the left exiting to a road.

Cross over and go on ahead through a Recreation Ground car park and on across fields exiting to pass to right of residences. At a road opposite Ablington Farm turn right and in 50m turn left up a farm track. Follow the farm track round for 200m and then turn right onto a track leading into a wooded shrubby area. Continue straight ahead crossing a farm lane and in 700m arrive at a track where turn right and in 5m turn left into a grassy area. Walk on bearing about 85 degrees across a military road and aim for the right-hand side of a detached house and on ahead to go between houses exiting at a road by a telephone box. Here turn right and in 20m turn left and go to the right of a gate by the side of a wood and on ahead crossing three fields exiting on a lane to the right of terraced houses.

Turn right and in 150m turn left along a tarmac footpath, cross the River Avon and at a T-junction turn left and follow the path until reaching the end of a lane. Here turn right and in 100m turn right along a footpath into a wooded area exiting over a stile into a field by Upper Farm. Cross the field on bearing about 150 degrees then cross over a stile into another field to follow the tree line on the left and up to a stile to cross to the other side of the hedge line. Here turn right and continue down the right-hand side of the field exiting at the right-hand corner to a lane. Continue on ahead exiting from Church Lane by St Leonard's church at Bulford. Cross over the road (A3028) and go through a gate opposite and across a grassy area to cross over a footbridge and stile then turn right. Keeping to the right hand edge of the field, enter a second field through a gap and exiting over a stile to a lane by 'The Dovecote'.

Here turn left and in 50m at a T-junction turn right onto a concrete lane. After 200m before a gate bear left up a footpath exiting through a gate and up to a track. Here bear left to follow a track across fields, just before electricity transmission lines, for a short distance, follow a parallel footpath on the left-hand side. In about 600m up to a junction where turn left onto a surfaced road. At a bend after 250m turn right at a bridleway sign onto a surfaced path to cross the A303(T) by a footbridge and up to Ratfyn Rd. Here turn right and after 400m arrive at a T-junction with London Rd, here turn right. In 400m cross over the A345 and into High St and up to a T-junction with Church St and Salisbury St in Amesbury.

Amesbury to Salisbury
16.3kms (10.0 miles) Time: 4.0 hrs

From the T-junction of Salisbury St, Church St and High St in Amesbury (**Map 25**) walk west along Church St soon crossing over the River Avon, where the road turns right into Stonehenge Rd go ahead up Recreation Rd. At its end by a car park turn right down a footpath to cross a series of footbridges over the River Avon and up to a junction of paths. Take the path on ahead (signposted 'Durnford') uphill at about 220 degrees. After 400m at a farm track continue ahead and up to a gate. Go through the gate and follow the left-hand fence uphill until the exit gate is seen to the right at the far end of the field, go through the gate and bear left. Keeping to the left-hand edge of the field continue on across for about 600m, crossing one track and on to SU1390 3920 where turn left onto a footpath and through a gate and in 100m to a track on the edge of Ham Wood.

Here turn left and in 500m down to a lane at SU1409 3857 where turn right. Follow the lane through to a T-junction in Great Durnford after 800m. Here turn left on a lane signed to 'Winterbournes' and after 1.2kms (0.75 miles) uphill to a T-junction where turn right. In 150m turn left on a concrete road. After 700m just after a left-hand bend pass through a gate on the right, at SU1352 3645, and proceed across fields with a fence on the right, on bearing about 210 degrees. After 700m cross a track and on ahead for a further 500m across another field to enter a small wood through a gate at a crosstrack (Monarch's Way). After 50m carry straight on through the wood to enter a field and on ahead passing Keepers Cottage in 800m. In a further 1.2kms (0.75 miles) pass Shepherds Corner and on ahead to a road after 600m. (**Map 24**)

Cross over the road and carry on ahead following a path between fences towards Old Sarum through two gates and up to a road entrance to Old Sarum. Here turn right and in 50m bear left through a gate and then immediately bear right to walk round the outer parts of Old Sarum. Pass through a gate and then in a further 120m turn sharp left downhill on a well-defined path through the trees. At a wooden gate at a T-junction turn left, and at a junction of paths by a wooden gate, turn right before it and carry on down to a road. Here turn right and in 200m turn left into Mill Lane. After 200m bear left onto a tarmac track to cross over the River Avon and up to a cross track after 100m.

Here turn left onto a gravel path eventually turning left again in 900m at the end of the gravel section to join the riverside path on a raised wooden footpath. Then on to a raised earth banking and at its end turn left over a footbridge over a stream and up to a road. Cross over the road and continue alongside the river under two bridges and across several roads. At Mill Stream Approach continue ahead alongside a coach park to regain the riverside path. At a point where the river goes underneath buildings go through an archway, on right, exiting to cross the river by a footbridge into Bridge St. Cross over the road and turn right and in 20m turn left alongside the river. At the next road bridge turn left into Crane St. Then turn right into High St to go through an arch and into Salisbury Cathedral grounds and on up to the Cathedral.

Collingbourne Kingston to Newbury

Map: OS Explorer 131, 157, 158
Start: St Mary C of E Church Collingbourne Kingston
Finish: Kennet and Avon Canal at Bridge St Newbury
Distance: 46.8kms (29.0 miles)
Time: 12.25hrs
Transport: Railway: Hungerford, Kintbury, Newbury
      Buses: Collingbourne Kingston (infrequent), Burbage,
Ramsbury, Hungerford, Kintbury, Newbury
Places of historical interest: Littlecote House, The Bear at Hungerford, Shaw
House Newbury (Previously part of the Trinity School now being renovated as a
tourist attraction)

The history

From Collingbourne Kingston the Prince detoured to Hampstead Marshall, to visit a stately mansion belonging to the Earl of Craven, reaching Hungerford in the late afternoon.

It was at Hungerford that King James's three Commissioners were to treat with Prince William. The three were the Marquess of Halifax, the Earl of Nottingham and the Lord Godolphin. The place of the meeting was at the 'Bear Inn' Hungerford. The terms offered to King James were as follows:

I That all Papists, and such Persons as are not qualified at Law, be Disarmed, Disbanded and Removed from all Employments civil and Military.

II That all Proclamations which reflect upon us, or have come to us, or declared for us, be recalled, and that if any persons for having so assisted us have been committed, that they shall be forthwith set at liberty.

III   That for the Security and safety of the City of London, the Custody and Government of the Tower be immediately put in the hands of the said City.

IV That if His Majesty should think fit to be in London during the Sitting of the Parliament, that we may be there also with an equal number of our Guards, or if his Majesty shall be pleased to be in any place from London, at whatever distance he thinks fit, that we may be at a place of the same distance. And that the retrospective Armies do remove from London 40 miles. And that no further forces be brought into the Kingdom.

V That for the Security of the City of London, and their Trade, Tilbury Fort be put in the hands of the said City.

VI That to prevent the Landing of French or other Foreign Troops, Portsmouth may be put into such hands, as by Your Majesty and Us shall be agreed upon.

VII   That some sufficient part of the publick Revenue be assigned us, for the Support and Maintenance of our Forces, till the meeting of a Free Parliament.

Given at Littlecot, Decemb. 9. 1688.

W.H. Prince of Orange'

The Prince who had been staying at the Bear Inn in Hungerford moved out to stay at Littlecote, as the inn was 'very unquiet'.

Sidney Godolphin, 1st Earl of Godolphin
By Sir Godfrey Keller, 1646-1723
© National Portrait Gallery

The King's commissioners replied to Prince William's terms:

'Upon consideration of the Princes answer, delivered by the Earls of Oxford and Shrewsbury and Monsr Bentinck, We offer to Hss that there are some particulars therein contain'd, to which We had power to have aggreed; But there are others of such a nature that are above our Commission to determine, wch makes it necessary that they should be presented to the King; And altho' the most expeditious way of knowing his mind might be to receive it by Expresse, Yet we conceive it may be more effectuall for Us to lay them before Him ourselves. In the mean time we propose that ye Prince will not permitt any of his Troopes to advance neare to London, than the distance of 30 sic miles mentioned in one of the articles of his Hss's paper, till after Thursday night, wch by our Computation is the soonest that an Answer can be returned.

Littlecott ye 10[h] of Decr 1688.

Halifax   Nottingham   Godolphin'

The three Commissioners then left the town.

The Prince of Orange went to 'Newberry' on this day. Reports claim he was at Shaw House, a Carolian mansion near Newbury.

The route: Eastbound

Commemorative Plaque at The Bear, Hungerford

Photo: L Ham

Collingbourne Kingston to Burbage 7.0kms (4.25 miles) Time: 1.75 hrs

From St Mary C of E church in Collingbourne Kingston (**Map 28**) walk north along the A338 towards Aughton. In 400m turn right on a footpath between hedges to Cuckoo Pen Close. Here turn left and into Ham Close and in 50m turn right down a lane. In 75m turn right and in 150m turn left through a gate and walk along a disused railway track for 2.3kms (1.5 miles) to SU2408 5862. Here turn left and in 250m up to a wood (Southgrove Copse) at SU2378 5875, here turn right alongside the wood. After 500m turn left through a gate and continue round the edge of

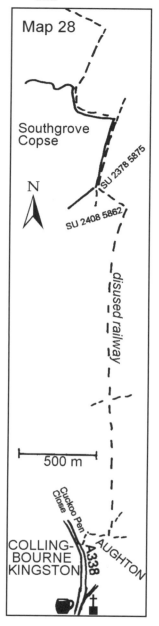

Map 28

Southgrove
Copse

N

SU 2378 5875

SU 2408 5862

disused railway

500 m

Cuckoo Pen
Close

COLLING-
BOURNE
KINGSTON

A338

LAUGHTON

Southgrove Copse. After 400m at a junction of paths by a stile turn right and follow a track between trees.

In a further 400m at a junction of farm tracks continue on the main track round to the left. And in a further 300m follow the track round to the right. Where the track turns right into a farm carry on ahead through a gate and up to the A338. Here turn left and in 20m turn right on a path marked 'Taskers Lane'. In a few metres one has to go through a gate and the grounds of a private house exiting through a gate and into a small field. At the right hand corner go over a stile to a cross path and on ahead alongside a hedgerow to the left-hand corner exiting over a stile to a surfaced footpath between residences and up to Suthmere Drive.

Here turn left and walk up to a T-junction where turn right. After 400m just past the White Hart public house turn right along a footpath crossing over Ailesbury Way and up to a T-junction of paths. Here turn left and in 20m turn right, follow this path round exiting to a lane opposite All Saints Church Burbage.

Burbage to Eight Walks crossroads, Savernake Forest 7.8kms (4.75 miles) Time: 2.0 hrs

Facing All Saints Church Burbage in Eastcourt turn left for 150m and walk to a T-junction where turn right. In 100m turn left and walk along Wolfhall Rd and after 1km at Wolfhall Farm turn left down a lane. In 200m where the lane becomes a track continue on ahead to the Kennet and Avon Canal at a bridge. Here turn left along the canal towpath for 1km to just before Bruce Tunnel where take the footpath on the left to a higher level and up to a road (Savernake Rd).

Here turn right along the road for just over 1km to Durley (**Map 29**). Just past a telephone box on the right turn left along a track leading to Savernake Forest. Follow this track for 1.3kms (0.75 miles) to a junction of tracks at the southern end of 12 o'clock Drive at SU2255 6440. As the name of the drive implies walk on bearing 0 degrees straight on and in 2.4kms (1.5 miles) arrive at Eight Walks crossroads in the centre of Savernake Forest at SU2255 6680

Eight Walks crossroads, Savernake Forest to Ramsbury
9.5kms (6.0 miles) Time: 2.5hrs

From Eight Walks crossroads at SU2255 6680 take the path east at 90 degrees. In 500m at SU2305 6683 turn left on bearing about 40 degrees crossing (Ashlade Firs Rd) after 250m. In a further 400m after crossing Amity Drive at a cross track at SU2349 6736 turn right on bearing about 130

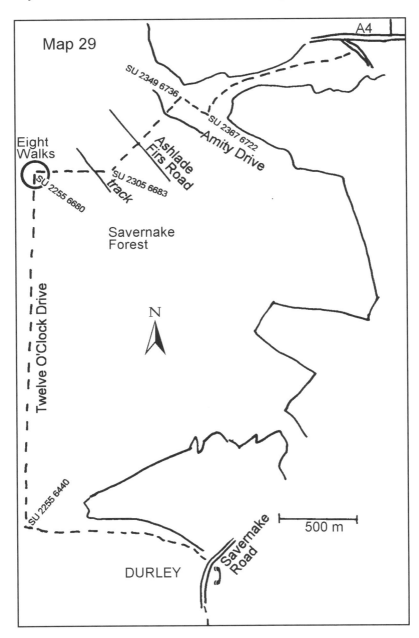

Map 29

SU 2349 6736

SU 2367 6722

Eight
Walks

Ashlade
Firs Road

Amity Drive

SU 2255 6680

SU 2305 6683

track

Savernake
Forest

N

Twelve O'Clock Drive

SU 2255 6440

500 m

Savernake
Road

DURLEY

A4

degrees for just over 200m to a point SU2367 6722. Here turn left, initially heading north the track swings east to parallel the A4 road in the valley on the left. After just over 1km walk up to a road, here turn left and in 150m arrive at the A4 road.

Turn right along the A4 and then crossing to the other side to walk along the grass verge. After 400m turn left up a track marked 'Ramsbury' and 'Hens Wood'. In 500m the track swings left and in a further 200m swings right at SU2475 6833. Maintain this path passing through a barrier in a northerly direction for 700m. In a dip where the gravel track swings left continue on a ahead on grassy uphill track.

At the top of the hill continue forward and enter a field through a gap at SU2485 6919. Cross the field marked on the OS map as 'The Plain' and 'Sky Close' on bearing 0 degrees to find a stile at SU2485 6970. Cross over the stile into a wooded area and go down to a cross track in 40m. Here turn right and in 40m at a Y-junction take the left fork downhill ignoring a crosstrack. Soon the River Kennet comes into view in the valley on the left. At the bottom of the hill at a cross track turn right to soon pass a cottage and to walk alongside the River Kennet.

Where the track joins a lane at a bend proceed on the surfaced lane ahead passing in front of residences. Before entering near residences do a short right and left and then maintain the same direction. Then go through a gate and between two cottages and on ahead and in 800m up to a lane.

(For those walkers not wishing to go into Ramsbury cross over the lane and continue on the path ahead, picking up the route description on line three in the Ramsbury to Hungerford text.)

Here turn left into Ramsbury. In 300m arrive at a T-junction at The Knap at SU2774 7161. *(The main village is to the left.)*

Ramsbury to Hungerford
8.5kms (5.25 miles) Time: 2.5 hrs

From the T-junction at The Knap SU2774 7161 walk south away from Ramsbury on a lane. In 300m before a hill, at a cross track of paths, marked 'Littlecote House' 2 miles (3.2kms), turn left. Maintain direction ahead ignoring other paths, after 1.1kms (0.75 miles) pass West Lodge residence. In a further 1.8kms (1.0 miles) pass Littlecote House. Continue along the road to exit to a road through the main inbound traffic gate by a lodge.

Note: It is possible to walk through the actual grounds of Littlecote House parallel to the route described but 50m to its left. This takes you past the house, hotel, and craft shops. Where the buildings end take the right fork marked with a 'no entry' sign for vehicles. This route brings you out 10m from the main inbound traffic gate as described above.

Here turn left and in just over 1km walk up to a T-junction with the B4192 at a bend. Here turn right up a concrete access track towards the Chilton Foliat Sewage Works. Just before the gate to the Sewage Works turn right on a path leading uphill into a wooded area. When the path levels out ignore a track from the right and in 100m Hungerford becomes visible in the valley on the left. Skirt round a residence (Kiln Cottage) to join its access track. Follow this track down the hill to the A4 road.

Cross over the A4 and turn left. In 150m turn right down a path then go over a stile into Freeman's Marsh. Cross over two footbridges then bear left and up to Marsh Lock on the Kennet and Avon Canal. Cross over the swing bridge and turn left. Follow the canal towpath up to the road bridge (A338) in Hungerford.

Littlecote Manor, Hungerford

Photo: L Ham

Hungerford to Newbury
14.0kms (8.75 miles) Time: 3.5 hrs

From the road bridge (A338) over the Kennet and Avon Canal walk along the towpath going east and continue for 1.5kms (1.0 miles) to Dun Mill Lock where cross over the bridge to the other side of the canal. Continue east and after a further 3.7kms (2.25 miles) arrive at Kintbury. And in a further 7.1kms (4.5 miles) at Guyers Lock cross over the bridge to the other side of the canal. Continue on towards Newbury and at West Mill cross over a swing bridge to the other side of the canal. In 500m after passing Newbury Lock and the Lock Stock and Barrel public house arrive at Newbury Bridge in Newbury.

The route: Westbound

Newbury to Hungerford
14.0kms (8.75 miles) Time: 3.5 hrs

From Newbury Bridge over the Kennet and Avon Canal walk west down a passage and walk past the Lock Stock and Barrel public house turning left after a few yards through a tunnel to the towpath. Turn right and go past Newbury Lock and up to a swing bridge across the canal. Cross over it to the other bank in West Mill. Walk along the westbound towpath and in 1.2kms (0.75 miles) reach Enborne Bridge where cross over to the other bank by

Guyers Lock. Continue on in the same direction for 7.1kms (4.5 miles) to reach Kintbury Lock, then continue for a further 3.7kms (2.25 miles) to reach a bridge at Dun Mill Lock. Here cross over the bridge to the other bank and in a further 1.5kms (1.0 miles) go up to Hungerford Bridge over the Kennet and Avon Canal.

Hungerford to Ramsbury
8.5kms (5.25 miles) Time: 2.5 hrs

From the road bridge (A338) over the Kennet and Avon Canal walk along the towpath in a westerly direction soon passing Hungerford Lock. At Marsh Lock cross over the swing bridge and go forward to cross two footbridges and a stile and up to the A4 road. Here turn left and in 150m turn right up an access track marked 'Kiln Cottage'. Skirt round to the right of the cottage and carry on ahead ignoring track on left. Go down the hill in a wooded area and round Chilton Foliat Sewage Works to join an access road and down to the B4192 at a T-junction on a bend. Here turn left along a road marked 'Littlecote House'.

Hungerford Bridge

Photo: L Ham

In just over 1km turn right on an access road to Littlecote. Continue on, passing Littlecote House. Where the road turns right to a visitor car park go on ahead and in 300m at a Y-junction continue on in the same direction.

(Note: It is possible to walk through the actual grounds of Littlecote House parallel to the route described above but 50m to its right. 10m short of the main inbound traffic gate bear right on a footpath between trees. This takes you past the craft shops, hotel and house. Once clear of the house go on ahead to rejoin the track as described above)

In 1.4kms (nearly 1.0 miles) pass by West Lodge near the River Kennet. In a further 1.1kms (0.75 miles) go up to a lane.

(For those walkers not wishing to go into Ramsbury cross over the lane and continue on the path ahead, picking up the route description on line three in the Ramsbury to Eight Walks crossroads text.)

Here turn right and walk up to a T-junction at The Knap in Ramsbury. (The main village is to the left)

Ramsbury to Eight Walks crossroads, Savernake Forest 9.5kms (6.0 miles) Time: 2.5hrs

From the T-junction at The Knap SU2774 7161 walk south away from Ramsbury. In 300m before a hill, at a cross track of paths, turn right along the track marked 'Mill Lane' 0.5 mile. After 800m go between two cottages and on ahead to go through a gate and on ahead. Maintain this direction for 900m making a few metres detour round a residential area to join a surfaced lane. Continue on and up to a sharp bend after passing residences on your left.

Here proceed along the track ahead soon walking alongside the River Kennet on your right. After 1.3kms (0.75 mile), and 100m after a cottage, turn left on a footpath leading uphill into a wooded area. Nearing the top of the hill at a Y-junction turn right and in 30m turn left up a track leading to a stile at SU2485 6970. Cross over the stile and into a field. Cross the field marked on the OS map as 'Sky Close' and 'The Plain' on bearing 180 degrees to pass the edge of a wooded area protruding into the field on the right. Continue in the same direction aiming for the bottom right-hand corner to exit the field through a gap at SU2485 6919.

In 30m take the left fork and go downhill for 300m to join a gravelled forest track. Proceed through Hens Wood in a southerly direction ignoring tracks to left or right. At a point SU2475 6833 the track swings left then in 200m right and down to meet the A4 road (**Map 29**). Here turn right and in 400m just past a lay-by, turn sharp left along a road.

In 150m turn right along a forest track on an arm of Savernake Forest. Proceed at about 255 degrees initially parallel to the A4 later to swing away to the left. At a main cross track at SU2367 6722 in just over 1km turn right along a track at about 310 degrees. In just over 200m where the track bends right at SU2349 6736 turn left along a track. In 400m having crossed Amity Drive arrive at a main cross track (Ashlade Firs Rd). Cross over the crosstrack and continue on a narrower track. In 250m at a crosstrack at SU2305 6683 turn right on bearing about 270 degrees. In 500m arrive at Eight Walks crossroads at SU2255 6680.

Eight Walks crossroads, Savernake Forest to Burbage 7.8kms (4.75 miles) Time: 2.0 hrs

From Eight Walks junction of paths in Savernake Forest at SU2255 6680 walk south along 12 0'clock Drive on bearing 180 degrees for 2.4kms (1.5 miles) to arrive at a crosstrack at SU2255 6440. Go forward on the track opposite soon bearing round to the left and in 1.3kms (0.75 miles) exit at a road (Savernake Rd). Here turn right and continue along the road and in just over 1km after crossing a railway bridge turn left along a track by a house. Go through a gate and down to the Kennet and Avon Canal. Walk alongside the canal for 1km to a bridge over the canal.

Here turn right along a lane away from the canal and on ahead, after 300m continue on the left main lane to a lane on a bend by Wolfhall Farm barns. Here turn right along the lane (Wolfhall Lane) to Burbage. After 1km go up to a T-junction where turn right along Eastcourt Rd. In 100m turn left into Eastcourt and in 150m arrive at All Saints Church Burbage.

Burbage to Collingbourne Kingston
7.0kms (4.25 miles) Time: 1.75 hrs

From All Saints Church Burbage cross over the lane and go along a footpath between residences round the edge of an enclosed grassy area. At a junction of paths turn left and in 20m turn right to continue over Ailesbury Way and on to the main road by the White Hart public house. Here turn left along the road and after 400m turn left into Suthmere Drive. Just after the T-junction with Ailesbury Way turn right down a footpath between residences. Cross over a stile and into a field continuing along the right-hand edge by a hedgerow. At a cross track go on ahead over a stile and into a small field.

In the left-hand corner go through a gate and pass through the grounds of a private residence exiting through a gate and up to the A338. Here turn left and in 20m turn right along a track marked 'Southgrove Copse'. Continue ahead to go through a gate and onto a farm track. The track bears round to the left and later turns right (**Map 28**) underneath power cables. In 400m go forward across a field and up to a wood (Southgrove Copse). Here turn left before it to go round the edge of the copse and in 400m up to a gate. Go through the gate and turn right and in 500m walk up to a cross track at the corner of Southgrove Copse at SU2378 5875.

Here turn left and in 250m go up to a disused railway. Here turn right and continue ahead to its terminal point after 2.3kms (1.5 miles). Exit through a gate to a lane where turn right into Aughton village. At a T-junction in 100m turn left and at another junction in 75m turn left into Ham Close. Go forward into Cuckoo Pen Close soon to go right on a footpath through a hedgerow to the A338. Here turn left and in 400m walk up to St Mary C of E church at Collingbourne Kingston.

Newbury to Abingdon

Map: OS Explorer 158, 170
Start: Kennet and Avon Canal at Bridge St Newbury
Finish: Abingdon Bridge
Distance: 39.2kms (24.5 miles)
Time: 10.0 hrs
Transport: Railway: Newbury, Didcot, Radley Nr Abingdon.
  Buses: Newbury, Chieveley, West Ilsley, Steventon, Didcot,
Abingdon
Place of historical interest: Shaw House Newbury (Previously part of the
Trinity School now being renovated as a tourist attraction). Commemorative
stone to William of Orange's passage over the 'Golden Mile' now situated inside
Harwell UKAEA at SU4724 8637 by the Fermi Gate, at the end of Fermi Rd.
East Hendred (Catholic Church attacked). A plaque commemorates William
having stayed at Mr Medleycott's house at 28 East St Helen St, Abingdon.

Commemorative Stone in the grounds of the UKAEA
With kind permission of the UKAEA

Special Note: For those wishing to visit the commemorative stone inside the UKAEA grounds please note that the UKAEA is a sensitive area and is on private land protected by CCTV cameras. If there are more than two or three walkers, or you wish to visit outside normal office hours, it is best to phone first. Please telephone (24hrs) 01235 820220 then ask for 'The Public Relations Manager' (in office hours) or 'The Duty Sergeant' at other times, advising them that you wish to visit the William of Orange commemorative stone.

The history

The Prince of Orange set off for Oxford on the 11th December where he was to meet with the heads of colleges who had earlier promised to support him. At this point the main body of William's army did not accompany him but would have marched directly to Reading. In Huygens journal he records:

'On the morning of Tuesday 11 December it was announced His Highness was going to Oxford, taking only very little luggage and expecting everybody else to do the same: so I took my bed loaded on my pack-horse. We marched to Abbington, a reasonably large town, where is a town hall with a large Italian portique, of hard-stone.'

His route north from Newbury would have taken him over the 'Golden Mile', a historic trading area, along the 'Old Hungerford Road', now a green lane and across Chilton Fields.

Inside the grounds of Harwell UKAEA there is a commemorative stone recording William's passage through the area, the plaque reads:

THIS IS ON THE SITE OF THE
ORIGINAL GOLDEN MILE OVER WHICH
WILLIAM OF ORANGE PASSED ON THE
11th DECEMBER 1688 ON HIS WAY
FROM HUNGERFORD TO OXFORD
ON THE JOURNEY TO LONDON TO
ACCEPT THE CROWN OF ENGLAND

In the village of East Hendred it is said that some of his (William's) men went to the Catholic Church as recorded by A L Humphreys in 1923:

"Philip Price was a Franciscan Friar who lived with the Eyston family (Hendred House) as Chaplain. It was while Price was Chaplain that the Chapel was desecrated. On the 11 Dec 1688 when the Prince of Orange was passing over the Golden Mile, a road near Hendred, on his way to Oxford, the Chapel was entered by some of the soldiers, who committed various acts of sacrilege. 'Some loose fellows came hyther went into the Chapel pretended to mock the priest by supping out of his Chalice, which they would have taken away had it been silver. Having torn down the 'Jesus Maria' from the altar, they retired taking an old suite of Church stuffe. This was all the mischief they then did, besides breaking the lamp and carrying away the Sanctus Bell."

At Abingdon the Mayor and Burgesses welcomed the Prince and paid 14s. 6d. (72.5p) to 'Ye ringers the day the Prince of Orange came to town' and £3.5s.9d. (About £3.29p) for 'sweetmeats upon treating the Prince of Orange'.

The Prince stayed at the house of a Mr Medleycott at 28 East St Helen St, Abingdon, a plaque records his visit. It was probably here where William heard that the King had left London. As recorded by Huygens:

'A man came from London – one of those merchants the French call quinqualiers (ironmongers) – came to His Highness to tell him that, as he also acted as a money-changer, on Monday evening many Irish officers had come to him to change gold. He, wondering what that might mean, went next morning at six o'clock to Whitehall, and learnt there from acquaintances that the King had left at four o'clock, to France, giving the order not to open the doors before 8 o'clock. That the Queen had already gone two days before the same way with the Prince of Wales.

These tidings caused so much joy at the court as one can imagine, but no confirmation had arrived when I left the court at half past ten that night.'

The route: Eastbound

Newbury to Chieveley
9.2kms (5.75 miles) Time: 2.5 hrs

From the bridge over the Kennet and Avon Canal in Bridge St walk along Bridge St and turn left into Northcroft Lane continuing past Northcroft Leisure Centre to follow the Lambourn Valley Way. Beyond the car park walk along the cycle way and footpath for 40m then turn left onto a lane. In 500m go under a railway arch then continuing on to the left of a house and into a field keeping to the right. In 250m turn right through two lines of hedgerows to go through a gate into a field at SU4560 6756. Cross the field due north and in 200m, at a gate and a lane, here turn left.

In 50m turn right by the church St Mary the Virgin, Speen, exiting through a lychgate continue on up to Speen Lane where turn left. At its terminal point cross over the A4 road and continue up the track opposite passing residences. Go through gates and onto a grassy track then into a field. Walk along the left-hand edge of the field by the hedgerow. Where the hedgerow goes left proceed ahead and then veer round to the right exiting to a wide gravelly track. Go forward for 70m to a road, cross over the road and go down the lane opposite. Where the lane bears right continue ahead alongside a fence by the A34. (**Map 30**)

Turn left by the River Lambourn under the A34 and up to a lane where turn right into Bagnor village. 100m after the Blackbird public house turn right between cottages signed 'public footpath' and enter a field. Cross the field uphill in the same direction to exit to a T-junction of paths, here turn left. In 800m walk to a junction at SU4562 7040. Turn left along a track and after 200m turn right up a surfaced private drive signed 'public footpath'. After 100m pass a residence at Honeybottom. Where the drive turns right behind the

Newbury Lock and Bridge

Photo: L Ham

residence continue forward to cross a step stile (with a chicken wire gate on top). Enter a field and turn right down a dip to follow the tree line up the right-hand edge of another the field. At the end of the tree line go forward into Withy Copse following the yellow waymarks. At a junction of paths turn right at a metal public footpath sign and in 40m go up to a metal gate. Cross over the step stile to its right and in 10m turn left to follow the line of the fence on the left. Maintain this path alongside the fence ignoring other paths and stiles over the fence. Exit through a metal gate and walk up to a lane at Winterbourne Holt at SU4596 7150.

Cross over the lane and make progress on a path in a northeasterly direction for 300m to a T-junction near Bussock Hill House at SU4622 7175, here turn left along a path called Pebble Lane. Follow this path ahead ignoring paths to left or right. After a downhill stretch and where the path turns left at SU4595 7239 turn right over a stile into a field. Cross the field and into another field steering half-right at about 70 degrees to a point at the corner of hedgerows where cross over a stile and in 200m reach a road (B4494) at Bussock Mayne.

Cross over the road and in 10m along the lane opposite turn left onto a path, then in 400m turn left along a path to cross over the M4 motorway on a footbridge and into a field. Turn right and follow the edge of the field to the end of the hedgerow. Proceed across a field and onto a lane and in 800m walk up to a T-junction with School Rd. Here turn right and in 40m arrive at a T-junction in Chieveley village.

Chieveley to West Ilsley
10.0kms (6.25 miles) Time:
2.5 hrs

From the T-junction at School Rd in Chieveley at SU4760 7385 turn left through Chieveley village and after 350m turn left into Manor Lane. In 100m

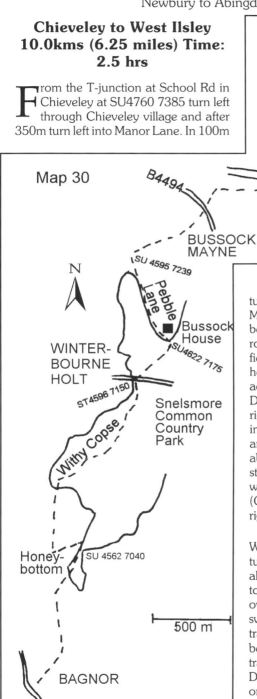

CHIEVELEY
School Road

Map 30

B4494

f.b.

M4

BUSSOCK MAYNE

SU 4595 7239

N

WINTER-
BOURNE
HOLT

Pebble Lane

Bussock House

SU4622 7175

ST4596 7150

Withy Copse

Snelsmore
Common
Country
Park

Honey-
bottom

SU 4562 7040

500 m

BAGNOR

A34(T)

turn right before Chieveley Manor and in 10m right again behind residences soon going round the left-hand edge of a field. At the end of the hedgerow continue on ahead across a field. After 800m at Downend turn left along the right-hand edge of a field and in 300m turn right over a stile and cross a field on bearing about 335 degrees. Exit over a stile by a wood after 800m, walk up to a cross track (Gridley Lane) and here turn right.

After 700m reach a lane at Woods Folly Bungalow, here turn left and in 50m turn right along a surfaced lane marked to 'Beedon Common'. In just over 200m where the lane swings right and becomes a track turn left up a track between hedgerows onto a track initially called 'Ilsley Down Riding Route'. Continue on ahead into 'Old Street Lane' path and after 1.7kms (1.0 miles) reach Hailey Lane. Cross over the lane and proceed on ahead onto 'Downland Villages Riding Route' between hedgerows. After 700m at a Y-junction by a centrally located tree at SU4663 7904 bear right initially at about 10 degrees. Follow the path round to the right and then go on a bearing of about 40 degrees along a track 'Green Lane' ignoring a path on the right. Continue on this byway between trees and on up to Redlane Barn after 600m.

Here proceed in the same direction and in 120m turn left down a path between trees continuing down a hill to open farmland and after 1.3kms (0.75 miles) at SU4751 8075 turn left down a path. In 50m at a Y-junction turn right along the 'Berkshire Circular Route' following the track round to a T-junction by Hodcott House, here turn right round Hodcott House turning right again at a gate and in 100m go down to a lane. Here turn left and where the lane turns right by Keepers Stables take the byway to the left between residences along Church Way. Exit at a road where turn left and arrive at All Saints Church opposite Bury Lane in West Ilsley.

West Ilsley to Steventon
11.5kms (7.25 miles) Time: 3.0 hrs

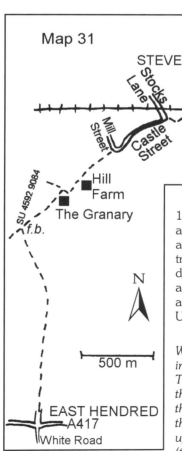

From All Saints Church in West Ilsley walk west out of the village and 100m after passing The Harrow public house turn right along a bridleway and after 450m ignore the track on the right and continue ahead uphill. Keeping to the left of the 'Race Horse Gallops' walk on ahead for 1.9kms (1.25 miles) to a junction of tracks and gallops at SU4622 8484. Here turn right across the gallops and across the 'Ridgeway' track and on ahead on bearing about 20 degrees. In 750m at a cross track continue on ahead along a track called 'Stileway Rd' alongside a security fence behind Harwell UKAEA on the right.

At this cross track if you wish to visit the William of Orange commemorative stone inside the UKAEA follow the instructions: Turn right along a track with the UKAEA on the left and continue for about 300m to go through a gate and on between fences exiting through another gate after a further 350m and up to a cross track. Here turn left for 1.4kms (the track becoming surfaced). After passing a school on the left and 50m before the end of the lane turn left along a road. In 300m go up to a junction where turn right along the Perimeter Rd. Follow the road round slowly bearing left for 600m, (passing a memorial stone, on the right, to the Airborne Forces who took off from here for Normandy in 1944) the road comes close to the A4185 then veers away again and up to a roundabout. Here turn left along Fermi Rd. Go to the end of Fermi Rd (about 1km) and at the police station at the Fermi Gate bear round to the right for 50m, the memorial stone is on the left at SU4724 8637. Return to the Orange Way by the reverse route.

Follow this path ahead for 2kms (1.25 miles) and up to a cross track at an entrance to Aldfield Farm. Here turn left along a concrete lane called 'Shadwell's Row'. After 300m turn right along a track by a wood and in 200m at a cross track continue on ahead to bear left in 30m. In 300m cross an entrance track go on ahead ignoring paths to left or right and in 400m follow the path down to the left exiting to a gravel path by cottages and up to a lane. Here turn right and up to a lane by a church, St Mary's East Hendred and St Patrick's East Ilsley. Here turn right along St Mary's Rd and walk up to a T-junction opposite the church of St Augustine.

Here turn right and go through East Hendred village along High St passing to the right of the war memorial and following the road round into White Rd (**Map 31**) and up to a T-junction with the A417. Cross over the road slightly left to go between residences and onto a track. Keep on ahead for 1.5kms (1.0 miles) to exit in the bottom left hand corner of the field through a difficult to see gap in the hedgerow and in 25m to cross a footbridge and stile and into a field. Here turn half-right to go between fences. Exit over a stile to another field and on ahead to another stile and field and up to Hill Farm exiting over a stile to a lane by The Granary.

Turn right and in 50m turn left along a footpath by a stream. Cross the field ahead exiting to a path alongside the stream and to a lane (Mill St). Turn right and follow the lane round to the left into Castle St. At the end of Castle St turn left into Stocks Lane and them immediately right onto a track. At its terminal point walk up to a road the B4017, here turn left across the railway bridge and into Steventon.

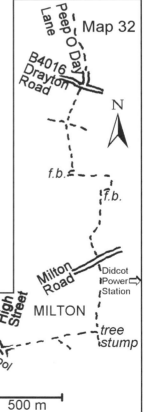

Steventon to Abingdon
8.8kms (5.5 miles) Time: 2.0 hrs

From the B4017 in Steventon walk in a southerly direction towards the railway. Just before the railway bridge turn left down Pugsden Lane. At the end of the residences the lane becomes a track. Follow this lane round to the left eventually becoming a surfaced lane again (Sheepwash Lane). At a junction with Kennet Lane continue on and in 60m turn right onto a cobbled footpath marked on the OS map as 'Milton Lane' (**Map 32**). Follow this up to the A34 (T) and cross over the footbridge continuing on in the same direction alongside a stream to skirt around Milton Manor. At a T-junction of paths turn right along an unsurfaced lane and on up to a road High St, Milton.

Here turn right and in 150m turn left up School Lane. Follow the lane round to the right and before Old Moor turn left up a lane (signed 'footpath') which soon becomes a track between tall bushes. Nearing the end of the track go left to exit a hedgerow and into a large field. Continue forward towards the eggcups of Didcot Power Station on bearing about 80 degrees. After 300m at a crosstrack by a small rotten tree stump turn left on bearing about 5 degrees and in 100m pass under power lines and later behind residences and on up to a road (Milton Rd).

Cross over the road and turn left and in 20m turn right on a footpath (signed 'Drayton 2'). Walk along the right-hand edge of the large field following the winding hedgerow to the very top right-hand corner ignoring gaps in the hedgerow. At the very top right-hand corner before a ditch turn right through a gap in the hedgerow and then immediately turn left over a wooden footbridge over a ditch and into another field.

Exit from this field is on the opposite side but we have to walk round the edge of the field.

Here turn right and keeping to the right-hand edge of the field walk to the corner and turn left, walk to the next corner and turn left again. Walk alongside a

Abingdon Town Hall

Photo: L Ham

Commemorative Plaque at 28 East St Helen's Street, Abingdon
Photo: L Ham

ditch for 300m and turn right over another wooden footbridge over a ditch and into a large field.

Turn right and in 50m ignoring the stile on the right cross the field ahead on bearing about 350 degrees to pass a cattle trough under a bush. Exit over a stile then cross a track and go over another stile into another field. Go on ahead aiming for a metal cattle trough on the other side of the field. Exit over a stile to the left of the cattle trough and keeping to the left-hand edge of the small field exit in the left-hand corner over a stile to continue on along an enclosed footpath by residences. Exit over a stile to a road, the B4016 Drayton Road.

Here turn right and in 50m turn left on a gravelled bridleway Peep O Day Lane and Cycleway Number 5. In 950m where the cycleway joins a lane on a bend continue along the lane in the same direction. After passing a sewage works (Thames Water), and Sports Ground on the left and gravel pits and Marina on the right exit Peep O Day* Lane to pass the end of Lambrick Way and on into West Quay. At the end of West Quay turn right into North Quay and in 25m turn left to follow Cycleway Number 5 along a short concrete path to go forward onto a road (Wilsham Rd) to draw and walk alongside the River Thames.

Continue along Wilsham Rd to its terminal point at a T-junction. Turn right over a bridge and along St Helen's Wharf. Follow the road round turning right into East St Helen St and up to a junction of roads in Abingdon at Market Place by the old Abingdon County Hall. Turn right into Bridge St and walk up to Abingdon Bridge in Abingdon.

The route: Westbound

Abingdon to Steventon
8.8kms (5.5 miles) Time: 2.0 hrs

From Abingdon Bridge walk into Abingdon along Bridge St and up to a junction of roads at Market Place. Turn left into East St Helen St passing the old Abingdon County Hall. At a T-junction opposite the Parish Church of St Helen, Abingdon turn left and proceed along St Helen's Wharf. Follow the road to a T-junction with Wilsham Rd. Here turn left along Wilsham Rd later

*   Author's note
In the 1780s a long tradition of sectarian faction fighting in Armagh, was formalised with the creation of the Catholic "Defenders" movement and the Protestant "Peep o' Day Boys". The "Peep o' Day Boys" were so called because they used to visit the houses of their opponents (Defenders) at the peep of day searching for arms or plunder. The outnumbered Catholics tended to get the worst of it and Catholic refugees, who fled into North Leinster and Connaught, brought their Defender affiliations with them and the movement spread. As it grew in size it became increasingly daring and explicitly political in its objectives. It demanded a republic. After a battle near Loughgall, Co Antrim in which thirty Defenders were shot dead, the Peep o' Day Boys formed the Orange Society, which later became the Orange Order.

leaving the River Thames to continue on to pass Andesey Way on the right and onto a concrete path signed National Cycle Path 5. After 60m exit to North Quay where turn right and in 25m at a T-junction turn left into West Quay.

At the end of West Quay pass the end of Lambrick Way to continue on along the concreted Peep O Day Lane (**Map 32**) (National Cycle Path 5) signed 'Didcot'. Continue ahead on the cycleway for 2kms (1.25 miles) passing Marinas on the left and Sports Fields, Sewage Works Thames Water and gravel pits on the right. Exit Peep O Day Lane at a T-junction with the B4016 Drayton Road.

Here turn right leaving the cycleway and in 50m turn left over a stile onto an enclosed footpath between residences signed 'Milton 2'. At the end of the hedgerow cross over a stile on the left and enter a small field. Walk along the right-hand edge exiting over a stile into a larger field. Cross the field ahead on bearing about 200 degrees exiting over a stile, across a crosstrack, and over another stile and into a field. Cross the field slightly left on bearing 170 degrees passing a small tree by a cattle water trough. At the bottom of the field ignore the stile on the left and continue round to the right for 50m to exit left over a wooden footbridge over a ditch and into a field.

The exit from this field is on the opposite side but we have to walk round the edge of the field.

Here turn left and follow the left-hand edge of the field alongside a stream. After 300m in the corner of the field turn right and at the next corner before a gap in the hedgerow turn right again. In about 50m turn left over a wooden footbridge and into a field. Turn immediately right and through a gap in the hedgerow and into a large field. Turn left and keeping to the left-hand edge of the field follow the hedgerow, ignoring gaps, to the very bottom of the field to exit by a residence at a road (Milton Rd).

Cross over the road and turn left and in 20m turn right on a footpath signed 'Milton ½'. Walk initially behind residences and continue in the same direction passing underneath power lines and in a further 100m look for a path on the right at a T-junction of paths by a small rotten tree stump. Here turn right and walk away from Didcot Power Station crossing the field on bearing of about 270 degrees. At a hedgerow go forward into it to join a path between high bushes. Soon passing residences on the right the path becomes a wide track and later a surfaced lane just before a T-junction at Old Moor. Turn right and follow the lane into School Lane to exit at a T-junction with High St Milton.

Here turn right and in 150m turn left on a bridleway (Mill Lane) round Milton Manor. Before the lane enters a residence in 600m, turn left on a footpath alongside a stream and up to the A34 (T). Cross over the footbridge and proceed in the same direction along 'Milton Lane' (**Map 31**) ignoring other paths. In 500m walk up to a lane amongst residences, here turn left and in 60m at a Y-junction take the right-hand lane (Sheepwash Lane). It soon becomes unsurfaced, then a track, follow it over a stream and round to the right and up to a lane (Pugsden Lane). At its terminal point arrive at a road the B4017 at Steventon.

Steventon to West Ilsley
11.5kms (7.25 miles) Time: 3.0 hrs

From the B4017 at Steventon walk in a southerly direction to cross the railway bridge. Turn immediately right on an unsurfaced lane alongside the railway. At its terminal point at Stocks Lane turn left and immediately turn right into Castle St. At the end of Castle St turn right into Mill St and in 20m after crossing a bridge, turn immediately left up a footpath alongside a stream. Exit to a field and continue on ahead to a lane at Hill Farm. Turn right and in 50m turn left by The Granary to cross over a stile.

Cross two fields over stiles and into a third field then bearing left after 50m exiting at SU4592 9084 over a stile and footbridge over a stream in a wooded area. In 25m exiting to a field and on ahead on bearing 160 degrees and up to a road (A417) after 1.5kms (1.0 miles). Cross over the road slightly left and into White Rd. Walk along White Rd and round into High St and through the village of East Hendred. Just after the church of St Augustine turn left along St Mary's Rd. At a T-junction by St Mary's and St Patrick's church turn left along a lane and in 80m turn left on a gravel track past cottages and on ahead up a track by a fence.

After 70m at a T-junction turn right uphill and continue on due south. After 400m cross an entrance track and in a further 300m to join a farm track and up to a cross track in 40m. Maintain same direction and after 200m walk up to a concrete lane (Shadwell's Row), here turn left. After 300m arrive at a junction before an entrance to Aldfield Farm, here turn right on a track bearing about 190 degrees and carry on ahead for 2kms (1.25 miles) passing Harwell UKAEA on the left to arrive at a cross track.

At this cross track if you wish to visit the William of Orange commemorative stone inside the UKAEA follow the instructions as previously described (page 134), but from this direction turn left first instead of right.

Proceed on ahead for 750m and up to another cross track (The Ridgeway) and racehorse gallops. Cross over the Ridgeway and racehorse gallops and turn immediately left on a track bearing round to the right alongside the racehorse gallops. At the end of the racehorse gallops continue on ahead down a track and down to a lane. Here turn left and in 400m arrive at to All Saints Church at West Ilsley.

West Ilsley to Chieveley
10.0kms (6.25 miles) Time: 2.5 hrs

From All Saints Church opposite Bury Lane walk east along the road for 200m and turn right up Church Way. At its end exiting by Keepers Stables to a lane where turn right. After 400m turn right up a bridleway and go through a gate after 100m and to the left round Hodcott House. After 200m turn left and follow the main track between hedgerows on the 'Berkshire Circular Route'. Follow the track round to the right and after 900m at a T-junction of paths turn left. In 50m at a T-junction of paths turn right and on ahead onto the 'Downland Villages Riding Route' ignoring a crosstrack after 200m. After 1.1kms (0.75 miles) to join a track where turn right and on to Redlane Barn. Maintain same direction along 'Green Lane' track ignoring track to left after 700m. At a T-junction take the path to the left and in 20m left again to join a path coming in from the right at a Y-junction with a centrally positioned tree at SU4663 7904.

Here follow the path ahead on bearing about 170 degrees, on 'Downland Villages Riding Route', to cross Hailey Lane in 700m. Maintain the same direction along 'Old Street Lane' and 'Ilsley Down Riding Route' path for 1.7kms (1.0 miles) exiting to a lane where turn right. After 200m walk up to a T-junction where turn left and in 50m turn right on a track by Woods Folly Bungalow. After 700m at SU4678 7581 cross over a stile on the left and into a field crossing it on bearing about 150 degrees exiting over a stile, here turn left. At the end of the field before houses at Downend turn right and cross a field, keeping to the left of a hedgerow. After 800m turn right before houses to exit to a lane (Manor Lane) by Chieveley Manor, here turn left and continue up to a road in Chieveley. Here turn right and in 400m arrive at a T-junction with School Rd in Chieveley.

Chieveley to Newbury
9.2kms (5.75 miles) Time: 2.5 hrs

From the T-junction in Chieveley at SU4760 7385 (**Map 30**) go down School Rd for 40m and turn left into a lane. At its terminal point continue ahead across a field to meet with a hedgerow on your left. Follow alongside the hedgerow round the field then turning left over a footbridge over the M4 motorway. Keep to the path ahead through a wood and up to a T-junction of paths where turn right. In 400m arrive at a lane where turn right. In 10m cross the B4494 road at Bussock Mayne taking the footpath to the right of the main gates. Exit over a stile to a field where cross slightly right at about 250 degrees. Exit over a stile to another field continuing ahead to exit over a stile to a footpath at SU4595 7239, here turn left uphill.

This path is called Pebble Lane, continue ahead ignoring paths to left or right. In 500m at a Y-junction keep to the right hand main path and in a further 200m at a T-junction near Bussock Hill House at SU4622 7175 turn right and in 300m arrive at a lane near Winterbourne Holt at SU4596 7150.

Cross over the lane and go through a metal gate into Snelsmore Common Country Park. Continue downhill into the wooded area following the yellow waymarks and alongside the fence ignoring stiles over it. At a Y-junction bear right to follow the fence. At a metal gate cross over the step stile to its left. Go downhill for 40m to a junction of paths by a metal public footpath sign. Here turn left and follow the path through Withy Copse exiting through a gap and into a field. Keeping the tree line on your left walk down the left-hand edge of the field. At the dip go forward up the next field for 60m to turn left over a step stile (*with a chicken wire gate on top*). Continue forward onto a private drive passing a residence at Honeybottom and in 100m to a cross track. Here turn left and in 200m walk up to a junction at SU4562 7040.

Turn right along the track for 800m watching for a stile in the hedgerow at SU4543 6960, here turn right over the stile and cross the field downhill to exit between cottages to a road. Here turn left through Bagnor village and in 300m, 30m after crossing the bridge over the River Lambourn turn left along a path to go under the A34 road. Follow the path round to the right and alongside the fence, exiting to a lane and on ahead up to a road. Cross over the road and go along the wide stony track opposite signed 'Lambourn Valley Way'. After 70m at a junction of paths go forward into a field bearing slightly left and uphill. Follow the path round to the left to join a hedgerow on the right. Exit in the top right-hand corner onto a grassy track by residences. In 40m go through gates onto a stony track and down to a road, the A4.

Cross over the A4 and on into Speen Lane. Walk along Speen Lane and in 230m turn right down a track and to a church lychgate (St Mary the Virgin, Speen). Follow the path through the churchyard to a lane, here turn left and in 50m turn right through a gate into a field. Turn right and cross the field on bearing about 180 degrees to exit through a kissing gate. Cross through two lines of hedges and into a field. Here turn left and in 200m go through a gate by a house. Continue on through a railway tunnel and along a lane ignoring paths or roads to left or right. At its terminal point in 500m turn right and in 50m turn left passing Northcroft Leisure Centre and on into Newbury by way of Northcroft Lane.

Section 12
Abingdon to Reading

(Sections 12 and 13 basically follow the Thames Path)

Map: OS Explorer 170, 171
Start: Abingdon Bridge
Finish: Caversham Bridge Reading
Distance: 49.9kms (30.75 miles)
Time: 12.75 hrs
Transport: Railway: Radley ((4kms (2.5 miles) from Abingdon)), Cholsey, Goring, Pangbourne, Tilehurst, Reading
     Buses: Abingdon, Culham, Clifton Hampden, Dorchester, Wallingford, Moulsford, Streatley on Thames, Goring,Whitchurch on Thames, Pangbourne, Purley on Thames, Reading
Places of historical interest: A plaque commemorates William having stayed at Mr Medleycott's house at 28 East St Helen Street, Abingdon; Reading (a skirmish took place here)

The history

On the 12th December the Prince of Orange changed his mind at Abingdon and went to Wallingford on this day, he had heard that the King had left London.

The Wallingford Town Council hired boats for £19:6:6 (£19:32½p) to carry the Prince to Windsor.

The Revd Whittle reported a skirmish at Reading between the two opposing armies:

'As part of our Regiments of horse were coming to Reading, the Irish Souldiers gave out great swelling Words, and lofty Speeches, how they would hack them to pieces there, and how they would defend the seven Bridges; This was the Lord's Day. (And as we were informed there, by divers Persons of Credit, they designed to massacre the People at their Worship, had they not been prevented) which obliged the Inhabitants to send to the advanc'd part of the Prince's Army, then a few miles distant, who readily came to their Assistance, being conducted a by-way into the Town, and fought so courageously, that in a few minutes they put the Irish to flight, took some, and kill'd about 20 upon the place, with the loss only of the Officer that led them, and the Guide that conducted them into the Town.'

The route: Eastbound

Abingdon to Day's Lock (Dorchester)
12.8kms (8.0 miles) Time: 3.25 hrs

From Abingdon Bridge over the River Thames on the A415, cross over the bridge walking away from Abingdon. Immediately over the bridge turn right to follow a path alongside the River Thames, on your right. In 1.4kms (0.75 miles) cross a footbridge over the Back Water then turn right. Then proceed alongside the River Thames for 2.0kms (1.25 miles) up to Culham Lock. Go past the lock and up to a gate at a road.

Cross over the road and a stile and continue on ahead. In 2.0kms (1.25 miles) pass underneath a railway bridge and in a further 2.5kms (1.5 miles) walk up to Clifton Lock. Go past the lock and in a further 700m arrive at Clifton Hampden Bridge, here turn right over the bridge and immediately left through a gate to regain the river. With the River Thames on your left carry on for 4.5kms (2.75 miles) and arrive at Day's Lock near Dorchester.

Day's Lock (Dorchester) to Wallingford
8.6kms (5.25 miles) Time: 2.25 hrs

After crossing Day's Lock turn right, and after 2.4kms (1.5 miles) turn left away from the river for 50m across a field and go up to the A4074. Here turn right along the A4074 for 600m (*beware of fast moving traffic*) to Shillingford. At Wharf Rd turn right for 400m and just before the end turn left up an enclosed footpath (*Note the River Thames high flood markings on wall*). After 40m at a T-junction turn right and in 250m join a drive, and on ahead and in 200m walk up to a road, here turn right and in 30m take the path to the left of Shillingford Bridge down to regain the River Thames.

Wallingford Bridge

Photo: L Ham

At the river turn left and continue downstream for 1.9kms (1.25 miles). Then immediately after a boatyard turn left for 40m across a field to the A4074. Here turn right and then immediately turn right down a side road for 400m. Then turn right down a path to cross the weir and Benson Lock. Across the lock turn left downstream with the River Thames on the left. After 1.9kms (1.25 miles) exit from Castle Lane to the High St at Wallingford Bridge.

Wallingford to Goring
10.8kms (6.75 miles) Time: 2.75 hrs

From the junction of Castle Lane and High St turn right for 30m then left into Thames St. Where the road swings right continue ahead towards the church. In 100m turn left down a passage round the back of the church exiting through an archway between terraced houses and into a lane. Here turn left and pass through a boatyard and on ahead. After 4.2kms (2.5 miles) at Cholsey Marsh Nature Reserve turn right along an unsurfaced track, later surfaced, away from the river and in 750m walk up to the A329 by Fair Mile Hospital.

Here turn left along Reading Road and in 800m cross over a railway bridge and on through Moulsford. In a further 1.6kms (1.0 miles) turn left down Ferry Lane to regain the river in 200m at the Beetle and Wedge public house. Here turn right. In 1.9kms (1.25 miles) pass Cleeve Lock and just short of Goring Lock turn half-right across a field exiting over a stile and footbridge to a lane. Continue round the back of the Parish Church of St Mary at Streatley on Thames and up to the B4009. Here turn left and cross the double bridge across the River Thames to Goring.

Goring to Whitchurch
7.1kms (4.5 miles) Time: 1.75 hrs

Having crossed the bridge to the Goring side of the Thames turn right down steps and right again to the river. Here turn left alongside the River Thames downstream, the river on the right. In 2.2kms (1.25 miles) pass under a railway bridge and in 400m at Ferry Cottage turn left and in 100m at a T-junction turn right. The path ascends to Hartslock Wood and then crosses a valley by way of steps and up to a drive by a farm entrance. Continue on ahead for 1.5kms (1.0 miles) to the B471. Here turn right through Whitchurch and after 500m turn right on a drive and walk up to the church. Go to the left of the church exiting by an enclosed path. In 25m turn left along a drive to rejoin the B471 by Whitchurch Bridge (tollbridge). Here turn right and cross the bridge.

Whitchurch to Reading
10.6kms (6.5 miles) Time: 2.75 hrs

Once across Whitchurch Bridge turn left into a car park at the Dolphin Centre, then left to the River Thames. At the river turn right alongside it. Follow the course of the River Thames through Pangbourne Meadow and after 3.6kms (2.25 miles) to Mapledurham Lock. Go past the lock and immediately enter a field. Turn right following hedgerow and up to a gate. Go through the gate and ahead onto Mapledurham Drive.

At the end of Mapledurham Drive where it joins Purley Village turn left and then right into New Hill. Walk up New Hill and over a railway bridge and then left into Hazel Rd. Turn right into Skerritt Way. At its end turn right up steps to the A329, here turn left. In 250m just before the Roebuck Hotel public house turn left down steps and cross the footbridge over the railway and on down to rejoin the River Thames. Here turn right maintaining the riverside path to Caversham Bridge.

The route: Westbound

Reading to Whitchurch
10.6kms (6.5 miles) Time: Time: 2.75 hrs

From Caversham Bridge continue upstream for 4.6kms (2.75 miles). Here turn left away from the river up steps and cross over the railway on a footbridge and up to the A329 by the Roebuck Hotel public house. Here turn right along the A329. After 250m turn right down steps between residences to Skerritt Way. Here turn left and up to Hazel Rd where turn left. Continue to its end at a T-junction and turn right into New Hill. Go over a railway bridge and in 120m at a T-junction turn left into Purley Village and immediately right into Mapledurham Drive.

At its end in 400m go through the right hand gate into a field and follow the left hedgerow to the River Thames. Here turn left into Mapledurham Lock. Go past Mapledurham Lock and continue upstream for 3.6kms (2.25 miles) to Whitchurch Bridge (tollbridge). Just short of the bridge turn left into a car park by the Dolphin Centre and exit on the right to the B471. Here turn right and cross the bridge.

Whitchurch to Goring
7.1kms (4.5 miles) Time: 1.75 hrs

Immediately after crossing Whitchurch Bridge turn left into a drive then right on an enclosed path to the church. Cross the churchyard passing to the right of the lychgate and to a drive. Here turn right to rejoin the B471. Here turn left and go through Whitchurch village and in 500m turn left along a drive. After 1.2kms (0.75 miles) where the drive turns left continue on ahead down steps and across a valley then through Hartslock Wood then descending to a broad track. Before Gatehampton Farm turn left and in 100m regain the River Thames by Ferry Cottage. Here turn right and continue ahead under a railway bridge and after 2.0kms (1.25 miles) walk up to the road bridge at Goring. Just before the bridge turn right then left up steps to the B4009 at Goring.

Goring to Wallingford
10.8kms (6.75 miles) Time: 2.75 hrs

From the two bridges at Goring cross over the River Thames to Streatley and in 80m turn right along a drive to the Parish Church of St Mary. Follow the drive round to the right and 50m beyond the church take the right-hand footpath. At its end cross over a footbridge and stile then crossing a field rejoin the River Thames. Here turn left and continue upstream passing

Cleeve Lock after 1.5kms (1.0 miles). Then after a further 2.1kms (1.25 miles) walk up to the Beetle and Wedge public house. Here turn left away from the river up Ferry Lane to the A329.

Here turn right through Moulsford and after 2.4kms (1.5 miles), turn right at a crossroads by Fair Mile Hospital. In 750m rejoin the Thames by Cholsey Marsh Nature Reserve. Here turn left and proceed upstream. After 3.4kms (2.0 miles) pass through a boatyard exiting between hedges to a lane. Walk along the lane then turn right down a passage between terraced houses to an enclosed path behind a church. At its end turn right into Wallingford by way of Thames St and up to the High St. Here turn right and in 30m turn left into Castle Lane by Wallingford Bridge.

Wallingford to Day's Lock (Dorchester)
8.6kms (5.25 miles) Time: 2.25 hrs

From the junction of High St and Castle Lane by Wallingford Bridge go down Castle Lane turning right in 20m to rejoin the River Thames and continue on ahead upstream. After 1.9kms (1.25 miles) reach Benson Lock. Cross the lock and weir and up to a road where turn left. In 400m at the junction with the A4074 turn left between hedges to regain the river in 40m. Here turn right passing through a boatyard and caravan park and after 1.9kms (1.25 miles) walk up to Shillingford Bridge.

Turn right along a path to the road. Proceed along the road away from the bridge for 30m then turn left down a driveway. In 200m where the drive divides take the footpath on the right behind residences. In 250m turn left at a T-junction by a cottage and in 40m arrive at a road (Wharf Rd). Here turn right (*Note the River Thames high flood markings on the wall*) and in 400m walk up to the A4074. Here turn left along the A4074 (beware of fast moving traffic) for 600m then turn left across a field for 50m to rejoin the River Thames. Here turn right and continue upstream to Day's Lock in 2.4kms (1.5 miles).

Day's Lock (Dorchester) to Abingdon
12.8kms (8.0 miles) Time: 3.25 hrs

Cross over Day's Lock and weir to the other side of the River Thames where turn right. With the river on the right maintain this bank for 4.1kms (2.5 miles) and up to the six arch brick built Victorian bridge. Exit to a road where turn right and cross the bridge. Immediately over the bridge turn left down a path to regain the river. Walk on ahead with the river on the left and after 700m arrive at Clifton Lock.

Go past the lock and in 2.5kms (1.5 miles) go under a railway bridge and in a further 2.0kms (1.25 miles) go up to a stile at a road. Cross over the road and go through a gate opposite and up to Culham Lock. Go past the lock and in a further 2.0kms (1.25 miles) turn left over a footbridge over Back Water to continue on ahead alongside the River Thames. In a further 1.4kms (0.75 miles) after passing a sports ground walk up to a road, the A415, at Abingdon Bridge.

Reading to Windsor

(Sections 12 and 13 basically follow the Thames Path)

Map: OS Explorer 171, 172, 160
Start: Caversham Bridge Reading
Finish: Eton Bridge Windsor
Distance: 53.1kms (33.25 miles)
Time: 13.5 hrs
Transport: Railway: Reading, Shiplake, Henley on Thames, Marlow, Bourne End, Cookham Rise, Maidenhead, Windsor
     Buses: Reading, Sonning, Shiplake, Henley on Thames, Marlow, Bourne End, Cookham, Maidenhead, Windsor
Places of historical interest: Reading (a skirmish took place here as described above), Phyllis Court, Henley on Thames (now a private members club); Maidenhead; Windsor Castle.

The history

The Wallingford Town Council hired boats for £19/6/6 (£19.32½p) to carry the Prince to Windsor. On the way he stayed at Phyllis Court, Henley, the home of Sir William Whitelock.

After leaving Reading William's army went by way of Tylehurstone to Maidenhead where the Revd Whittle records:

'At Maidenhead as we heard there from a Worthy Divine. The Irish perceiving the Army of the Prince of Orange advancing so fast, and with such speed towards London, perswaded the late King James to fortify Maidenhead-Bridg, it being a ready Road, and a difficult Post to be taken. Therefore a new Brick House which is built between the Bridg and the Town, they made sundry Port-holes for their great Guns, and put new Pales to blind them, and sundry places above to shoot with Musquets: And on the middle of the Bridg, they planted a great Gun or two, and here they were resolved to maul the Prince's Army, as they said. Indeed those that understood Fortification well, have presumed, that the Passage there might be so fortified, that thousands of Men should not win it, because the Water ran in the Road-way a considerable length, or some hundred Yards: and the Bridg is so narrow, that a Man can hardly go along without falling, except he hold by the Rails: ; the Water too being up to a Man's middle here in the Road at the lowest Ebb: so the Irish bravadoing here at this Post, what they should do, certain worthy Persons there consulted together how to disperse the Irish, or cause them to go away, for they perceived well the Hearts of all Protestants were set upon his Highness, their Deliverer, under God, and by his Blessing: and the End of their Consultation was this: Sundry Persons of

Courage and Resolution should go in the Dark, about Midnight, having each of them an old Barrel, or an old Kettle, standing at a certain equal distance from each other, they should beat the Dutch March: Which Stratagem took good effect, for these Men being got within a small distance of the Irish, began to beat a Dutch March: They no sooner heard it, but were prodigiously surprized, crying, Hark, Hark; and another presently made answer, God damm my Blood if it not be the Dutch come upon us; and forthwith they began to run and hasten away, without minding their great Guns or taking away any thing; nay, happy was the Man that could get before his Comrade; and wither they went, no Man could tell. So the Souldiers belonging to his Highness, coming to Maidenhead, hearing of this Exploit, highly commended both the Contrivers and Actors in it, brought away the Guns, and all that was left, to Windsor Castle.'

The route: Eastbound

Reading to Sonning
5.7kms (3.5 miles) Time: 1.5 hrs

From Caversham Bridge continue on downstream and after 800m pass under Reading Bridge, then past Caversham Lock. In a further 1.25kms (0.75 miles) cross over a footbridge at the mouth of the River Kennet. Keep on ahead alongside the River Thames and after passing Sonning Lock, arrive at Sonning Bridge after 3.5kms (2.25 miles).

Sonning to Henley
10.0kms (6.25 miles) Time: 2.5 hrs

Cross over Sonning Bridge and turn immediately right over a footbridge to proceed along the opposite riverbank. Follow the path ahead through fields for 2.6kms (1.5 miles) then enter a wooded area. Re-emerging into fields again to cross a footbridge by the Shiplake College Boathouses. Maintain the riverside path for a further 1km exiting through a gate by a flint wall. Here turn left up to a lane then turn right for 30m and then left onto a footpath across a field. Exit in the left-hand corner over a stile and across another field. Exit over a stile and up steps to a lane. Here turn left and in 50m reach a T-junction. Here turn right and continue on Mill Rd to a crossroads with Station Rd by the Baskerville Arms public house. Here turn right up to Shiplake railway station.

Cross over the railway level crossing and in 15m turn left down a footpath alongside the railway. After 150m at a junction of footpaths take the right-hand one through a gate then between residences to join a road. Here turn left and continue to its terminal point by Bolney Court. Take the footpath to the left of the gate and proceed keeping left to cross over a stream and into a field. Continue on ahead to regain the riverside path. Continue on to cross a long wooden footbridge to an island passing through Marsh Lock, then across a second long wooden footbridge, then to regain the riverbank. Here turn right and on into Henley and up to Henley Bridge by the Angel public house.

The Angel at Henley Bridge

Photo: L Ham

Henley to Aston
5.1kms (3.25 miles) Time: 1.25 hrs

Walking away from the town, cross Henley Bridge then turn immediately left and left again on a footpath to regain the River Thames by the Leander Club (*Phyllis Court is on the opposite bank*). Follow the footpath ahead to pass by Temple Island after 2.4kms (1.5 miles) and in a further 1.5kms (1.0 miles) reach Hambleden Lock. Go on ahead for 800m up to Ferry Lane where turn right away from the river. In 400m arrive at a T-junction by the Flower Pot public house at Aston.

Aston to Marlow
9.5kms (6.0 miles) Time: 2.5 hrs

From the junction with Ferry Lane and Aston Lane by the Flower Pot public house walk along Aston Lane and in 60m turn left along a lane into Culham Court Estate and into a wooded area. Where the lane turns right continue on ahead on a footpath to cross a sloping field and then pass in front of Culham Court. Exit to a field and on into a second field exiting through a gate and onto a track where turn left. Pass a farmhouse and after 250m at a junction of tracks turn left through a gate and cross a field diagonally left on bearing about 65 degrees to regain the riverside, here turn right.

Follow the riverside path passing Hurley Caravan Park and in 3.5kms (2.25 miles) cross a footbridge to an island to pass through Hurley Lock. Then cross a second footbridge to regain the riverbank where turn left and continue on ahead. In 800m cross another footbridge to the other bank and on through Temple Lock. In a further 2.2kms (1.5 miles) up to Marlow Bridge where turn left before the bridge and up to the High St. Cross over the road and arrive at the Parish Church of All Saints, Marlow.

Marlow Bridge and the Parish Church of All Saints
Photo: L Ham

Marlow to Maidenhead
12.8kms (8.0 miles) Time: 3.25 hrs

From the Parish Church All Saints, Marlow take the footpath through the churchyard going eastbound exiting an enclosed path to St Peter's St. Here go diagonally right and down another enclosed footpath between red brick walls. Exit this path into Mill Rd where turn right and after passing Marlow Lock and at a point where Mill Rd meets Gossmore Lane turn right down Lock Road Footway. Shortly regaining the riverside path to soon pass under a road bridge (A404). Continue on alongside the river through several fields, then through Spade Oak Meadow to exit by a railway crossing point.

From Spade Oak Meadow follow the footpath for 950m along the River Thames between residences, then passing through Upper Thames boatyard and Bourne End Marina. Continue along a narrow enclosed footpath and up to a railway bridge and footbridge across the River Thames. Here turn right up the steps and cross the river. At the foot of the steps on the other bank turn right underneath the bridge and continue alongside the river, now on your left. In a further 1.63kms (1.0 miles), just short of the road bridge over the river into Cookham, take the path on the right alongside a red brick wall and go through the Holy Trinity churchyard. Exit into Church Gate, turn left and in 20m turn right.

Follow the road round passing the High St and the Stanley Spencer Gallery on your right. Then on ahead into Sutton Rd and after 120m turn left down Mill Lane. In 460m turn right down the footpath opposite Sol Mill. Follow the path ahead ignoring paths to right and left and after 700m regain the River Thames, here turn right.

High on the opposite river bank is Cliveden, once the home of the Astor family, it was a meeting place of politicians and international celebrities, the so called 'Cliveden Set', before the Second World War.

Continue on this path eventually meeting with Lower Cookham Rd. Then after passing Boulters Lock walk along Ray Mead Rd and in 1km arrive at Maidenhead Bridge on the A4.

Maidenhead to Windsor 10.0kms (6.25 miles) Time: 2.5 hrs

At Maidenhead Bridge turn left and cross over it walking away from the town then immediately turn left and left again into a boatyard to pass under Maidenhead Bridge to cross the A4. Continue along the river edge to join River Rd soon going underneath Brunel's railway bridge. Then continue on ahead passing

Holy Trinity Church, Cookham
Photo: L Ham

Cookham Village
Photo: L Ham

Bray Lock after 2.25kms (1.5 miles) and Boveney Lock in a further 4.75kms (3.0 miles). On approaching Windsor, after crossing a field, go through a gate and onto a private road for 40m then into Brocas St and up to Eton High St, here turn right and up to Eton Bridge at Windsor.

The route: Westbound

Windsor to Maidenhead
10.0kms (6.25 miles)
Time: 2.5 hrs

From Eton Bridge walk towards Eton into Eton High St and turn immediately left into Brocas St. Passing the Waterman's Arms public house and through a short private road to a field. Cross the field with the River Thames on the left and follow the riverside footpath passing Boveney Lock after 2.5kms (1.5 miles) and in a further 4.75kms (3.0 miles) Bray Lock. In a further 2.25kms (1.5 miles) and after passing under Brunel's railway bridge and along River Rd, then go left to the river edge and underneath Maidenhead Bridge to cross the A4. Immediately turn right out of the boatyard and right again to cross the bridge towards Maidenhead.

Maidenhead to Marlow
12.8kms
(8.0 miles)
Time: 3.25 hrs

From Maidenhead Bridge on the A4 facing towards the town turn immediately right into Ray Mead Rd. Walk along Ray Mead Rd and at Boulters Lock (1km) continue into Lower Cookham Rd. In 250m bear right maintaining riverside path for 2.2kms (1.25 miles) where turn sharp left away from the river.

High on the opposite river bank is Cliveden, once the home of the

Boulters Lock, Maidenhead

Photo: L Ham

Astor family, it was a meeting place of politicians and international celebrities, the so called 'Cliveden Set', before the Second World War.

Ignore paths to left or right and in 700m reach Mill Lane opposite Sol Mill. Here turn left and in 450m up to Sutton Rd, here turn right into Cookham village.

Brunel's railway bridge and Maidenhead Bridge beyond

Photo: L Ham

Walkers at Spade Oak Meadow

Photo: L Ham

Go past the Stanley Spencer Gallery and the High St and after following the road round soon taking a left turn into Church Gate. Turn immediately right into the Holy Trinity Church, crossing the churchyard to the left of the church, exiting to regain the riverside path, here turn left. In 1.6kms (1.0 miles) cross over the River Thames by a footbridge on the far side of the railway bridge. On the opposite bank turn left. Proceed ahead for 950m with the River Thames on the left. Then passing through Bourne End Marina and Upper Thames Boatyard and on to Spade Oak Meadow with a railway crossing on the right.

Cross Spade Oak Meadow going on ahead alongside the River Thames across several fields. Then pass underneath a road bridge (A404). On approaching Marlow Lock bear right between residences to Mill Rd where it meets Gossmore Lane. Here turn left to pass Marlow Lock. 150m after a bend turn left along an enclosed footpath between red brick walls. Exit to St Peter's St where cross diagonally right to go down another enclosed footpath and into the churchyard of the Parish Church of All Saints Marlow. Go through the churchyard exiting to the High St at Marlow.

Marlow to Aston
9.5kms (6.0 miles) Time: 2.5 hrs

From The Parish Church of All Saints Marlow cross over the High St and take a footpath on the left in front of Tierney Court, Riverside, and down to the river at Marlow Bridge. Here turn right and walk westbound alongside the River Thames. After passing through Temple Lock cross over the footbridge to the other bank and on ahead. In 800m re-cross part of the Thames to an island over a footbridge to walk through Hurley Lock, re-crossing over another footbridge back to the riverbank and on ahead.

At a Y-junction of paths take either one and in 1.5kms (1.0 miles) turn left diagonally across a field on bearing about 245 degrees leaving the river to join a track. Here turn right and after passing farm buildings take the left-hand track and in 50m go through a gate on the right to cross a field and into a second field. Exit to cross in front of Culham Court and on across sloping fields to enter a wooded area. Soon joining a track down to a T-junction with Aston Lane. Here turn right and up to a T-junction with Ferry Lane by the Flower Pot public house.

Aston to Henley
5.1kms (3.25 miles) time: 1.25 hrs

From the Flower Pot public house walk down Ferry Lane to its terminal point at the River Thames, here turn left. In 800m pass through Hambleden Lock and on past Temple Island after a further 1.5kms (1.0 miles). Then on alongside the Henley Regatta rowing course for 2.4kms (1.5 miles) (*Phyllis Court is on the opposite bank*) and up to a road by Henley Bridge. Here turn right and cross the bridge into Henley.

Henley to Sonning
10.0kms (6.25 miles) time: 2.5 hrs

From the Angel public house by Henley Bridge walk along Thames Side to regain the River Thames and on ahead for 1.4kms (1.0 miles) where turn left over a long wooden footbridge to an island. Walk through Marsh Lock and then across another long wooden footbridge to regain the riverbank. Walk alongside the river for 800m and then veer off to the right away from the river. Follow the path behind residences to join a road by Bolney Court. Proceed ahead bearing left at a fork and in 450m bear right onto an enclosed footpath between residences as far as a railway line. Here turn left alongside the railway line and up to a road where turn right over a railway level crossing at Shiplake.

Continue on the road ahead and just past the Baskerville Arms public house turn left down Mill Rd and in 700m turn left at a junction opposite Crowsley Rd. In 50m turn right down steps and go over a stile into a field. Go on ahead to cross over a second stile into another field. Here turn right exiting to a lane where turn right. In 30m turn left and then turn right through a gate before a footbridge to regain the riverside path. In 1km cross over a footbridge by Shiplake College Boathouses. Then continue on alongside the river for 3.5kms (2.25 miles) to cross a footbridge and up to a road where turn left and cross Sonning Bridge at Sonning.

Sonning to Reading
5.7kms (3.5 miles) Time: 1.5 hrs

From Sonning Bridge walk towards Sonning village then immediately over the bridge take the footpath on the right and continue alongside the River Thames upstream. After 500m pass Sonning Lock and in 3.0kms (1.75 miles) at the junction of the Thames and Kennet rivers cross the footbridge over the River Kennet. Proceed alongside the Thames for 2kms (1.25 miles) passing Caversham Lock, Reading Bridge and up to Caversham Bridge at Reading.

Windsor to Brentford

Map: OS Explorer 160, 161, 172, 173, and the London A-Z from Slough.
Start: Eton Bridge Windsor
Finish: Grand Union Canal at London Rd, Brentford
Distance: 26.0kms (16.25 miles)
Time: 6.5 hrs
Transport: Railway: Windsor, Slough, Langley, Iver, West Drayton, Hayes, Brentford
                Buses: Windsor, Slough, Langley, Iver, West Drayton, Hayes, Brentford
Places of historical interest: Windsor Castle, Syon House Brentford

---

The history

At Windsor, the Revd Whittle tells us:

'His Highness being now at Windsor, with all his Nobility and Gentry about him, the Citizens of London flock'd mightily to visit Him, and congratulate his safe Arrival so far.'

William was very concerned, as he had been throughout the March that his troops should behave in a proper manner towards the people and properties. This was also extended to the acquiring of food for the army as the Revd Whittle points out:

'The Army being now all about Windsor and the adjacent Towns and villages, the Souldiers, through the perswasion of the Country People, kill'd and destroy'd hundreds of Deer in the Forest: and hundreds more had been destroy'd, if so be his highness had not given out his Royal Order to the Contrary.'

On the 18th December Prince William left Windsor and journeyed to London but first stopping at Syon House, Brentford where he dined.

The route: Eastbound

Windsor to West Drayton
14.0kms (8.75 miles) Time: 3.5 hrs

From Eton Bridge over the River Thames proceed straight on ahead into Eton along the High St passing Eton College and after 1 km turn right on footpath at the Upper Club playing fields. After 200m just before where the path goes over a bridge (*do not cross*) turn almost about and take the right-hand footpath away from the bridge on bearing about 70 degrees to a road, the B3026. Cross over the road and continue ahead through Agars Plough and up to a suspension bridge over the River Thames Flood Relief Diversion at Myrke. Once over the footbridge turn immediately left along a path and at its end up to a road by a bridge under the M4 motorway.

Windsor Castle

Photo: L Ham

Go under the M4 motorway and continue into Slough along Windsor Rd. Cross over the High St and walk ahead along William St and on up to the A4 road. Cross over the A4 road via a subway exiting by the bus station to walk north along Stoke Rd. Continue over the railway bridge by Slough railway station and in 600m, and 50m before the road junction with Shaggy Calf Lane, turn right to join the Slough Arm of the Grand Union Canal at its terminal point. Follow the right-hand side of the canal and continue on ahead for 8.0kms (5.0 miles) to the junction with the Grand Union Canal. Cross over the footbridge and turn right along the Grand Union Canal, the canal on the right. After 800 metres go up to a bridge at High Street/Horton Rd, Yiewsley/ West Drayton.

West Drayton to Brentford
12.0kms (7.5 miles) Time: 3.0 hrs

From the bridge over the Grand Union Canal at the junction of High St, Yiewsley/West Drayton and Horton Rd take the footpath on the left-hand side of the canal going east. In 4.5 kms (2.75 miles) cross over Bulls Bridge at the Paddington Arm of the Grand Union Canal and on ahead to arrive at Norwood Lock. In a further 3.0 kms (1.75 miles) descend past the Hanwell flight of locks to arrive at Osterley Lock. After passing Osterley lock and under the M4 the River Brent joins from the left. Then continue on ahead to go under a railway bridge and then cross a footbridge to the other side of the canal, passing Clitheroe Lock, and on ahead. Go underneath the A4, then a railway bridge and through a covered canal boat-unloading bay. Continue on the towpath ahead and shortly arrive at Brentford Gauging Lock and on up to London Road, Brentford.

To visit Syon House turn right along London Rd and in 200m just after Field Lane on the right, turn left down a short road for 50m and go through gates into Syon Park and on ahead to Syon House.

The route: Westbound

Brentford to West Drayton
12.0kms (7.5 miles) Time: 3.0 hrs

From London Road, Brentford and the bridge over the Grand Union Canal take the footpath on the left-hand side of the canal soon passing Brentford Gauging Locks. Continue on ahead underneath a covered canal boat loading area, exiting and then going under a railway bridge and soon under the A4 road bridge. Then pass Clitheroe Lock and after 1.5kms (1.0 miles) from Brentford cross over a footbridge to the right-hand side of the canal.

Proceed on ahead passing under a high span railway bridge and underneath the M4 motorway. The River Brent comes in immediately on the right, carry on ahead passing Osterley Lock and after a further 2kms (1.25 miles) start to pass by the Hanwell flight of locks and up to the Norwood top lock in 1.3kms (0.75 miles). After a further 3kms (1.75 miles) meet the Paddington Arm of the Grand Union Canal on the right at Bulls Bridge, then in a further 4.5kms (2.75 miles) arrive at High St/Horton Rd, Yiewsley/West Drayton.

The flight of locks at Hanwell

Photo: L Ham

West Drayton to Windsor
14.0Kms (8.75 miles) Time: 3.5 hrs

From Grand Union Canal at High St/Horton Rd, Yiewsley/West Drayton continue along the right-hand side of the canal in a westerly direction. After 800 metres cross over a footbridge and join the Slough Arm of the Grand Union Canal going off to the left. Walk along the left-hand side of the Slough Arm for 8.0kms (5.0 miles) to the basin at its terminal point. In a further 20m at Stoke Rd turn left. Proceed along Stoke Rd passing Slough railway station and bus station and up to the A4 road. Cross the A4 by subway and maintain the same direction into Slough along William St. Cross over the High St and into Windsor Rd.

Continue down Windsor Rd and under the M4 motorway and immediately turn left along a path by the side of the River Thames Flood Relief Diversion. Proceed on to a footbridge at Myrke where turn right to cross it and enter 'Agars Plough'. Go forward along a path between lines of trees and up to a road (B3026). Cross over the road and enter 'The Playing Fields'. On approaching a brick bridge (*do not cross*) turn sharp right away from the bridge and go between a sports pavilion and a cricket field and up to a road (B3022) by the Upper Club. Here turn left into Eton passing Eton colleges and entering Eton High St and up to the pedestrianised Eton Bridge over the River Thames at Windsor.

Syon House, Brentford

Photo: L Ham

Brentford to St James's Palace London

Map: OS Explorer 173, London A-Z **Start:** Grand Union Canal at London Rd, Brentford **Finish:** St James's Palace London **Distance:** 20.0kms (12.5 miles) **Time:** 5.0 hrs **Transport:**   Railway: Brentford, Kew Bridge, Barnes Bridge, then trains buses and London underground in various places **Places of historical interest:** Syon House Brentford, Kensington Palace, Rotten Row and St James's Palace London

The history

It was at Kensington Palace that Prince William lived with his wife as King William III and Queen Mary II. He was brought here by carriage from Hampton Court after his riding accident and it was where he died as a result of it a few days later (see below).

On the 18th December 1688 the Prince of Orange arrived at St James's Palace having travelled through the parks of London to avoid the crowds. He was now back on familiar territory as he had been married at St James's Palace on the 4th November 1677.

The Prince's entry into London was recorded by the Revd Whittle:

'December the 18th, his Highness parted from Windsor, dined at Sion-House, and came that Evening to St. James's, amidst the loud Acclamations of a vast number of People of all Sorts and Ranks, the Bells everywhere ringing: the Evening concluded with vast Bonfires, and such general Joy as can scarce be parallel'd.'

Macaulay's account written in later Victorian times is as follows:

Whilst the King's barge was slowly working its way on rough waves down the river, brigade after brigade of the prince's troops marched into London from the West. It had been wisely determined that the duty of the capital should be chiefly done by the British soldiers in the service of the State General. The three English regiments were quartered in and around the Tower, and three Scottish regiments in Southwark. In defiance of the weather, a great multitude assembled between Albemarle House and St. James's Palace to greet the Prince. Every hat, every cane, was adorned with an orange ribbon. The bells were ringing all over London. Candles for an illumination were disposed in windows. Faggots for bonfires were heaped up in the streets. William however, had no taste for crowds and shouting, took the road through the park'

The Revd Whittle continues:

'Most of the Nobility congratulated his Highness's safe arrival at St. James's, and on the 20ᵗʰ the Aldermen and Common Council of the City of London attended his Highness upon the same account, and the Lord Mayor being disabled by Sickness, Sir George Treby, Kt Recorder of the Honourable City of London, made an Oration to his Highness to this effect: Great Sir. When we look back to the last Month, and contemplate the swiftness and fulness of our present Deliverance, astonish'd, we think it miraculous. Your highness led by the hand of Heaven, and call'e by the Voice of the People, has preserved our dearest interest, the Protestant Religion, which is Primitive Christianity restored. Our Laws, which are our ancient title to our Lives, Liberties and Estates, and without which this World were a Wilderness. But what Retribution can we make to your Highness? Our hearts are full charged with Gratitude.

Your highness has a lasting Monument in the Hearts, in the Prayers, in the Praise of all good Men amongst us. And late Posterity will celebrate your ever-glorious Name, till Time shall be no more.'

The route: Eastbound

Brentford to Hammersmith
12.0kms (7.5 miles) Time: 3.0 hrs

From Brentford High St at the bridge over the Grand Union Canal go down the steps on the south side of the bridge marked 'Thames Path'. Walk along the left-hand towpath soon gaining a higher level past houses and a timber yard. Exit at a road and ex-railway bridge. Turn sharp right under the bridge and regain the path up a stepped slope. After 100 metres cross over a footbridge to the right-hand side of the canal and continue up to Thames Lock. Go up the steps to the road (Dock Rd) and turn left over the bridge. Follow the road up to Brentford High St where turn right for 500m.

At a T-junction with Ealing Rd turn right down broad steps and in 20 metres go through a gap gate in a wall and turn immediately right. Follow the path round offices and up steps to regain riverside path. Go through Waterman's Park on the left bank of the Thames and up to the High St. Turn right for 70m and then immediately beyond a public house turn right to regain the riverside path. Walk alongside the River Thames and under Kew Bridge to join Strand on the Green then forward, shortly regaining the riverside path.

The path joins Grove Park Rd after a railway bridge. Continue along Grove Park Rd and fork right into Hartington Rd. Eventually at Chiswick Quay, turn right and after 130m take a footpath on the right behind residential buildings to briefly regain the riverside. At a lock cross over the lock gates (*take great care*) and turn left and in 30m turn right into Ibis Lane. Turn left up Ibis Lane to Hartington Rd. Turn right and up to Great Chertsey Rd.

Here turn right and cross Chiswick Bridge. Turn right down steps to the riverside and turn right under the bridge joining Thames Bank. Continue along the right-bank of the River Thames passing the Ship Inn public house. Pass under Barnes railway bridge and keeping to the riverside path up to Hammersmith Bridge. Here turn right before the bridge and up to the road. Here turn left and cross Hammersmith Bridge. Turn left into Rutland Grove and immediately right into Bridge View and up to the A4. Cross the A4 underneath Hammersmith flyover and on ahead into Bridge Ave and up to King St in Hammersmith.

Hammersmith to St James's Palace
8.0kms (5.0 miles) Time: 2.0 hrs

From the corner of Bridge Ave and King St, Hammersmith cross over King St and turn left. In 30m turn right into Leamore St. At Glenthorne Rd turn right and then second left into Southerton Rd, second right into Adie Rd and up to Hammersmith Grove. Turn left and right into Trussley Rd and underneath a railway arch. At a T-junction left into Sulgrave Rd and then first right into Batoum Gardens and up to Shepherd's Bush Rd. Here turn left and then right into Blythe Rd then second left into Addison Gardens, and on over a railway bridge into Lower Addison Gardens. Immediately after the bridge, turn right into Elsham Rd and left into Russell Gardens and right along Holland Rd.

Bear left into Addison Crescent (*not sharp left, which is also Addison Crescent*), cross over Addison Rd into Oakwood Court and up to Abbotsbury Rd. Turn left and in 50m go right through Abbotsbury Gate and into Holland Park. Pass tennis courts on the right, then just beyond children's playground on the right and toilets on the left, turn left on a main path. Follow the path round

Kensington Palace, London

Photo: L Ham

to the right in front of
Holland House, and exit
at a gate, crossing
Holland Walk into an
access road opposite.
Then continue into
Duchess of Bedford's
Walk, cross Campden
Hill Rd into Holland St,
cross Hornton St and up
to Kensington Church St.
Here cross on the pedes-
trian crossing into York
House Place and on
ahead through an access
passage into Kensington
Palace Gardens. Go
half-left into an access
road crossing Palace Ave
and entering Kensington
Gardens through a gate
then passing in front of
Kensington Palace on
the left. Proceed on
ahead with the round
pond on the left. Just
past the Serpentine Gal-
lery on the left, cross Exhibition Road and into
Hyde Park continuing on
in the same direction to
the right of Rotten Row.

St James's Palace, London
Photo: L Ham

A plaque alongside Rotten Row states:

Rotten Row the King's Old Road completed in 1690. This ride originally formed part of King William III carriage drive from Whitehall to Kensington Palace. It was the first lamp-lit road in the Kingdom, designated as a public bridleway in the 1730's.

Continue to the end of Rotten Row at Hyde Park Corner and cross over the pedestrian crossing across South Carriage Drive. Go through the gates by the Hyde Park Corner Lodge and cross over Knightsbridge by two pedestrian crossings. Walk through the Wellington Arch and cross two more pedestrian crossings and ahead along Constitution Hill to pass the Memorial Gates in 40m. Just beyond the Memorial Gates, fork left along a tarmac path into Green Park. After 120m, at the first cross path, turn right and continue for about 500m passing two ornamental lamp posts on the right, to exit from Green Park to a broad path. Turn left and in 60m turn right through an access gate and passageway to Cleveland Row. Turn right, then left, and up to St James's Palace on your right.

Congratulations. You have arrived!

The route: Westbound

St James's Palace to Hammersmith
8.0kms (5.0 miles) Time: 2.0 hrs

From the entrance to St James's Palace (Pall Mall/Cleveland Row) walk west along Cleveland Row then keeping to the left of Selwyn House go round right and left to a narrow access passage to Green Park. Here turn

left on a broad path and after 60m turn right, then after 15m, fork right, leaving an ornamental lamppost on your left. After 250m, pass a similar lamppost on your left, and then after 250m at the next cross path, turn left. This leads up to the Memorial Gates in Constitution Hill. Bear right to pass the Memorial Gates and cross over two pedestrian crossings, through the Wellington Arch, across two more pedestrian crossings. Having crossed Knightsbridge enter Hyde Park through a gate by the Hyde Park Corner Lodge, just past the gate.

Cross the South Carriage Drive by a pedestrian crossing then turn left to walk along a

William III statue, Kensington Palace, London
Photo: L Ham

tarmac path and cycleway to the right of Rotten Row.

A plaque alongside Rotten Row states:

Rotten Row the King's Old Road completed in 1690. This ride originally formed part of King William III carriage drive from Whitehall to Kensington Palace. It was the first lamp-lit road in the Kingdom, designated as a public bridleway in the 1730s.

After 1.3kms (0.75 miles) cross over Exhibition Rd and into Kensington Gardens. In 40m at a Y-junction, with the Serpentine Gallery on your right, take the left-hand path, passing Albert Memorial and Albert Hall on the left and, later, the round pond on the right, heading towards Kensington Palace. After passing the front of Kensington Palace exit by a gate and cross Palace Ave continuing on ahead on an access road to Kensington Palace Gardens.

Here cross the road half-left and go along a passageway to the left of Arundel House and into York House Place. After 200 metres cross Kensington Church St half-left into Holland St. Walk along Holland St crossing Hornton St.

Cross over Campden Hill Rd and go slightly right into Duchess of Bedford's Walk. At its extremity go through an access road crossing a footpath (Holland Walk) and enter Holland Park by a gate opposite.

Pass in front of Holland House, and then follow the path downhill to the left for a few metres and then turn right between public toilets and children's playground. Proceed on to an exit gate in Abbotsbury Rd. Here turn left and in 50m turn right down Oakwood Court. Cross over Addison Rd and ahead into Addison Crescent.

Bear right into Holland Rd and in 70m turn left into Russell Gardens and first right into Elsham Rd. At a T-junction with Lower Addison Gardens turn left and cross a railway bridge into Addison Gardens. Continue along Addison Gardens to the end, and then turn right along Blythe Rd and up to Shepherd's Bush Rd.

Here turn left and then right first into Batoum Gardens. At a T-junction, turn left into Sulgrave Rd, then first right into Trussley Rd and under a railway arch. Follow the road round to Hammersmith Grove where turn left and in 80m turn right into Adie Rd. Take second left into Southern Rd and at a T-junction, turn right into Glenthorne Rd, then first left into Leamore St and under a railway bridge and up to King St, Hammersmith. Turn left and in 30 metres turn right to Bridge Ave.

Hammersmith to Brentford
12.0kms (7.5 miles) Time: 3.0 hrs

From Bridge Ave and King St, Hammersmith walk along Bridge Ave and cross the A4 underneath a flyover and into Bridge View crossing Rutland Grove and up to Hammersmith Bridge. Cross the bridge on the right hand side and immediately take the footpath on the right down to the river. Turn left and continue ahead with the River Thames on the right. After 1.5kms (1.0 miles) the path joins alongside Lonsdale Rd. Continue along concrete path alongside the river and under Barnes railway bridge. Maintain the riverside path up to Chiswick Bridge. Go underneath the bridge and immediately turn left up the steps to the road. Turn left and cross the bridge.

After 250m turn left along Hartington Rd. In 200m turn left into Ibis Lane and go to the end turning right through an access passage to a lock. Turn left and cross the lock gates (*take great care*). Then on ahead along the riverside and then follow the path round behind houses into Chiswick Quay and on back up to Hartington Rd. Turn left and at the junction with Grove Park Rd turn left along it. In 130m take the path on the left alongside the River Thames and along Strand on the Green. Pass underneath Kew Bridge and eventually up to High St, Brentford and here turn left.

In 70m take the path on the left through Waterman's Park and regain the riverside path. Continue to the end of Waterman's Park regaining the High St opposite Ealing Rd. Turn left and after 500m turn left into Dock Rd and up to the Thames Lock on the Grand Union Canal. Turn right down the steps and go past the lock and on alongside the canal, on the right. After 200m cross over a footbridge to the opposite side of the canal and up to Brent Way. Go underneath an ex-railway bridge where immediately turn sharp left. Follow the path and take a lower level path up to a bridge at London Rd, Brentford.

To visit Syon House turn left along London Rd and in 200m just after Field Lane on the right, turn left down a short road for 50m and go through gates into Syon Park and on ahead to Syon House.

Postscript

William accepted the Declaration of Rights passed by the Convention Parliament, which met on 22 Jan 1689 and on 13 Feb 1689 William was crowned King William III, his wife Mary, became Queen Mary II and were proclaimed joint sovereigns of England. They reigned together until 1694 when Mary contracted smallpox and died, William then reigned alone for eight more years.

In February 1702 William was riding at Hampton Court when his horse, Sorrel, stumbled on a molehill and threw him, breaking his collarbone. After it

Queen Mary II

By William Wissing 1656-1687
© National Portrait Gallery

had been set, he insisted upon returning to Kensington Palace by coach, which aggravated his condition. He became feverish some days later and was put to bed but died of pleuro-pneumonia a few days later. He is buried in Westminster Abbey.

William III was: William I of Ireland; William II of Scotland; William III of England and William IV of Normandy.

As King William III of England he accomplished far more for the welfare of the English people than had most of his native born predecessors. He reformed the nations political and financial institutions. His reign marked the transition from the personal government of the Stuarts to the parliamentary rule of the Hanoverians, control of the army was transferred to Parliament, a better system of finance was introduced and the Bank of England was established. The constitutional rights of the people were set on a firmer basis. William throughout his reign was a dedicated advocate of tolerance.

Selected further reading

Appleyard J   *William of Orange and the English Revolution*
Ashley M   *The Glorious Revolution*
Burnet G Rev   *History of His Own Time*
Burnet G Rev   *A Complete History of the Glorious Life and Actions of William III*
Chacksfield M K *The Glorious Revolution, 1688*
Chapman G   *A History of Axminster to 1910*
Delderfield E R *Kings & Queens of England and Great Britain*
Green E   *The March of William of Orange*
Howarth M   *A Plain Man's Guide to the Glorious Revolution*
Humphreys A L   *East Hendred, A Berkshire Parish Historically Treated*
James D   *History of England*
Johnson D R   *William of Orange's Expedition to England*
Macaulay T B   *History of England*
Osborne J   *Hampton Court Palace*
Over L   *The Story of Maidenhead*
Pinkham L   *William III and the Respectable Revolution...*
Powley E B   *The English Navy in the Revolution of 1688*
Pulman G P R   *The Book of the Axe*
Sheppard E   *Memorials of St James's Palace*
Speck A W   *Reluctant Revolutionaries*
Speke H   *Some Memoirs of Remarkable Passages 1709*
Speke H   *The Secret History of the Happy Revolution in 1688*
Whittle J   *An Exact Diary of the Late Expedition of his Illustrious Highness, the Prince William of Orange, from his Palace at The Hague, to his Landing at Torbay, and from thence to his Arrival at Whitehall.*
Wright G N   *Roads and Trackways of Wessex*
Ogilby's   *Map C. 6. D. 8. (British Library)*

Useful addresses

Tourist Information Centres – (some are summer opening only Apr-Sep)

Devon

The Old Market House, The Quay, Brixham, TQ5 8TB
Tel: 0906 680 1268 (premium charge rate) Fax: 01803 852939

The Town Hall, Coronation Rd, Totnes, TQ9 5DF
Tel: 01803 863168/865771 Fax: 01803 865771

6 Bridge House, Courtenay St, Newton Abbot, TQ12 2QS
Tel: 01626 367494

Civic Centre, Paris St, Exeter, EX1 1JJ
Tel: 01392 265700 Fax: 01392 265260

10b Broad St, Ottery St Mary, EX11 1BZ
Tel: 01404 813964

Dowell St East Car Park, Dowell St, Honiton, EX11 1LT
Tel: 01404 43716

Old Court House, Church St, Axminster, EX13 5AQ
Tel: 01297 34386

Other information: www.eastdevon.net

www.exeter.gov.uk

Dorset

3 Tilton Court, Digby Rd, Sherborne, DT9 3NL
Tel: 01935 815341

Other information: www.westdorset.com

Somerset

www.southsomerset.gov.uk

Email: tourism@southsomerset.gov.uk

Crewkerne Tourist Office, Market Sq, Crewkerne, TA18 7LE
Tel: 01460 73441

Petter's House, Petter's Way, Yeovil, BA20 1SH
Tel: 01935 462991/2 Fax: 01935 434065
Email: yeoviltic@southsomerset.gov.uk

7 Carrington Way, Wincanton, BA9 9JS
Tel: 01963 34063

Wiltshire

Fish Row, Salisbury, SP1 1EJ
Tel: 01722 334956

Redworth House, Flower Lane, Amesbury, SP4 7HG
Tel: 01980 622833 Fax: 01980 625541
Email: amesburytic@salisbury.gov.uk

The Square, Mere, Warminster, BA12 6JJ
Tel: 01747 861211 Fax: 01747 861127

Berkshire

The Wharf, Newbury, RG14 5AS
Tel: 01635 30267

Windsor Information Centre, 24 High St, Windsor, SL4 1LH
Tel: 01753 743900

Maidenhead Information Centre, Maidenhead Public Library, St Ives Rd, SL6 1QU
Tel: 01628 796502

Marlow Area Information Centre, High St, Marlow, SL7 1AU
Tel: 01628 483597

Town Hall, Blagrave St, Reading, RG1 1QH
Tel: 0118 956 6226 Fax: 0118 939 9885

Oxfordshire

25 Bridge St, Abingdon, OX14 3HN
Tel: 01235 522711 Fax: 01235 535245

Town Hall, Market Place, Wallingford, OX10 0EG
Tel: 01491 826972

The Barn, Kings Rd, Henley on Thames, RG9 2DG
Tel: 01491 578034

Middlesex

Central Library, 14/15 High St, Uxbridge, UB8 1HD
Tel: 01895 250706 Email: clibrary@hillingdon.gov.uk

Britain Visitor Centre, 1 Regent St, Piccadilly Circus, London, SW1Y 4XT
Email: BVCCustomerServices@bta.org.uk

County Councils

Devon

Devon County Council, County Hall, Topsham Rd, Exeter, EX2 4QD
Tel: 01392 382000
www.devon.gov.uk
E-mail: info@devon.gov.uk

Dorset

Dorset County Council, County Hall, Dorchester, DT1 1XJ
Tel: 01305 251000
www.dorset-cc.gov.uk

Somerset

Somerset County Council, County Hall, Taunton, TA1 4DY
Tel: 01832 355455
www.somerset.gov.uk
E-mail: info@somerset.gov.uk

Wiltshire

Wiltshire County Council, County Hall, Bythesea Rd, Trowbridge, Wilts, BA14 8JN
Tel: 01225 713000
www.wiltshire.gov.uk

Berkshire

West Berkshire Council Offices, Market St, Newbury, RG14 5LD
www.westberks.gov.uk

West Berkshire Countryside Environment, Council Offices, Faraday Rd, Newbury, RG14 2AF
Email: webinfo@westberks.gov.uk

Oxfordshire

Oxfordshire County Council, County Hall, New Rd, Oxford, OX1 1ND
Tel: 01865 792422
Footpath Rights of Way Tel: 01865 810226
www.oxfordshire.gov.uk

Middlesex (there is no Middlesex County Council)

Hounslow Borough Council, Civic Centre, Lampton Rd, Hounslow, TW3 4DN
Tel: 020 8583 200
www.hounslow.gov.uk

Ealing Borough Council, Perceval House, 14-16 Uxbridge Rd, Ealing, W5 2HL
Tel: 020 8579 2424
www.ealing.gov.uk

Royal Borough of Kensington and Chelsea, The Town Hall, Hornton St, London, W8 7NX
Tel: 020 7937 5464 Fax: 020 7938 1445
Email:informationservices@bkc.gov.uk

Westminster City Council, Westminster City Hall, 64 Victoria St, London, SW1E 6QP
Tel: 020 7641 6000 Fax: 020 7641 3776
www.westminster.gov.uk

Buses
Devon

Devonbus

Tel: 01392 382800
E-mail: DevonBus@devon-cc.gov.uk

Stagecoach Devon Ltd, Bus Station, Paris St, Exeter, EX1 2JP
Tel: 01392 427711 or 01803 664500

Kilmington Coaches (Hawkchurch, Tipton St John)
Tel: 01823 672247

Sewards Coaches, (Dalwood, Axminster)
Tel: 01404 881343

Dorset

First Southern National
www.firstsouthernnational.co.uk

Bridgeport Office, 18 South St, Bridport, Dorset, DT6 3NQ
Tel: 01308 422080
And at: Edward St, Weymouth, Dorset, DT4 7DN
Tel: 01305 783645

Somerset

First Southern National
www.firstsouthernnational.co.uk

Tower St Bus Station, Taunton, TA1 4AF
Tel: 01823 272033

And at: Yeovil Bus Station, Glovers Walk,
Tel: 01935 476233

Wiltshire

Wilts and Dorset Bus Company, Travel Office, Bus Station, Endless St,
Salisbury, SP1 1DW
Tel: 01202 673555 or 01722 336855
Email: enquiries-salisbury@wdbus.co.uk

Badgerline Bus Company, Bus Station, Manvers St, Bath, BA1 1XX
Tel: 01225 464446

Wiltshire Bus Line
Tel: 08457 090899
E-mail: buses@wiltshire.gov.uk

Berkshire

Newbury Bus Company
Tel: 01635 567500

Oxfordshire

Stagecoach South Midlands, Horspath St, Cowley, Oxford, OX4 2RY
Tel: 01865 772250 Fax: 01865 747879
Email: info@stagecoach-oxford.co.uk

Middlesex

www.londontransport.co.uk
Tel: 020 7222 1234
Email: travelinfo@tfl.gov.uk
www.stagecoach-london.co.uk

Rail Services

National Rail Enquiry
Tel: 08457 484950
www.railtrack.co.uk

South West Trains
Tel: 0345 484950
www.southwesttrains.co.uk

Thames Trains Customer Service
Tel: 0118 908 3678

Travel information

for bus, coach and rail services throughout England, Wales and Scotland

Traveline
Tel: 0870 608 2608
Textphone: 0870 241 2216
www.traveline.org.uk

Other useful web sites

English Tourist Board: www.travelengland.org.uk

Weather in the UK by region and town: www.weather.co.uk;
    www.metoffice.com/weather/europe/uk/

The Rambler's Association: www.ramblers.org.uk

National Rail: www.nationalrail.co.uk

Public transport information, UK: www.pti.org.uk/

Streetmaps: www.streetmap.co.uk/

Business information (useful for finding taxis):
    www.scoot.co.uk/business/index.asp?

Index of Towns and Villages